Heartfelt

A Memoir of
Camp Mystic Inspirations

Claudia Sullivan

EAKIN PRESS ✦ Fort Worth, Texas
www.EakinPress.com

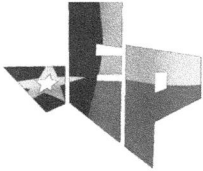

Library of Congress Cataloging-in-Publication Data
Sullivan, Claudia.
    Heartfelt : a Camp Mystic memoir of inspirations / Claudia Sullivan.
    1st ed.
        p.   cm.
    Includes bibliographical references (p.) and index.
        ISBN 1-57168-550-2
        1. Christian life. 2. Sullivan, Claudia. 3. Camp Mystic (Tex.) I. Title
    BV4501.3 .S85   2001
    248.4–dc21   2001005851

For Momma and Daddy,
my first teachers of Spirit

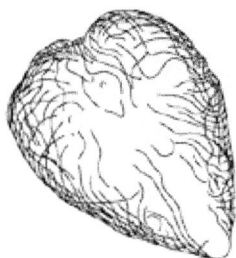

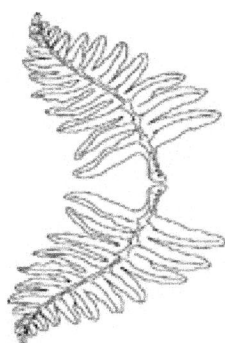

Contents

Acknowledgments

By nature of the form, a memoir owes more to those who have had significant influence on the writer than, say, a novel. A memoir is memory; therefore, I am indebted to all those who had an impact on remembered moments from the past. Many will go unnamed. None will go unforgotten.

Specifically, I owe thanks to the following:

Inez and Frank Harrison, for shaping the place and me;

Fr. Michael Boulette, for teaching me to trust and love the Lord;

Mary Ann Collins, for teaching me to listen to the Word;

Roby Conner, for his editing skills;

David Smith, who, because of his own camping experience, created sensitive and thoughtful designs that appear on the cover of this book and on chapter headings;

Evelyn Latimer, my mother, who insisted I go to camp and allowed me to return, year after year;

And especially good friends, good listeners, good writers, and those who paved the way.

On the banks of the Guadalupe River
there is the camp of my dreams
Where the whippoorwill calls softly
and the bright moon beams.

On the banks of the Guadalupe River
our hearts are loyal and true
Camp Mystic I will pledge
my true and faithful love to you.

All scripture entries are from the King James version of the Holy Bible. Although this is not the version I use currently in my personal meditations, it is the Bible I used in childhood, and therefore is part of my memory.

Introduction

Summer does not come subtly in the Texas Hill Country. It is a land uneasy with snow and sleet, chill factors, and dormant earth. The Hill Country is, however, a mixture of the tropical and subtropical, of arid plateaus and occasional blue northers that freeze the land for twenty-four hours or less.

The short days of fall and even shorter days of winter can be confusing. Eighty degrees at Christmas: "This feels like summer!" Forty degrees at Easter: "When will summer ever get here?" Then, without escort, summer arrives. Heat-loving flowers bloom; cicadas hiss; azure, cloud-filled skies break your heart; and warm winds blow from the four corners of the earth. In summer the Hill Country is in its glory.

We are a peculiar mix of Deep South gentility, southwestern individuality, Texas friendliness, and Mexican mystery. We are what the rest of the state calls "God's country." But I was not always familiar with this land, its inherent loveliness, its warm winds and immense skies. Nor did I understand the healing powers of summer. I was a city girl, born in Fort Worth, Texas. Fort Worth may have been for some "where the West begins," but during the 1950s and 1960s it was just another booming Texas city, its citizens struggling to discern the difference between being "southern" and "western."

I learned about summer before I went to public school. That important lesson came from my grandparents, who lived on a farm in the Piney Woods of Northeast Texas. From my grandparents I learned about life and love and being loved. I

1

learned how to spit watermelon seeds, how to bottle-raise an orphaned calf, and how to pick wild berries at their peak.

I furthered my summertime education when I first came to the Texas Hill Country, to summer camp, to Camp Mystic. Deep lessons came from my experiences at camp. There I learned about faith, about community, and about relationship: relationship with nature, with God, and with other people. The sum of these lessons has served me well through almost half a century. And, like any good student, I sometimes revisit my original instruction. That is the purpose of this book: to revisit the lessons I learned in the past in hopes that I may pass on to others some of what was shared with me.

The memories of summer have long been with me, cropping up in the most peculiar moments and for the most unusual reasons. I see a face, I hear a bit of music, the wind blows through the trees in a certain way ... and I am in another time and place. It is a reverie evoking a season full of hope, innocence, and endless energy.

I admit this is not a corporate recollection of sweet summer memories or tales of summer-camp adventures. Neither is it a diary of humorous anecdotes that will bring smiles to the lips of fellow "Kiowas" and "Tonkawas" scattered throughout the country. It is a personal journey through a time that, like the name of the camp, was filled with *mysticism*.

Mysticism ... I am not sure that I completely understood the term, or do now. Mysticism ... "at one with the spirit." What spirit? The spirit of life? Of nature, or of God? Mysticism ... "peacefulness of the cosmos" ... "a coming together of mind, body, and being."

I had my first glimpse, my first experience with mysticism in those days of summer some thirty-five years ago, in that place in the hills of Texas, hidden from the glare of urban life and parental strife.

Many American youngsters attend summer camp. I came out of that common experience, yet I had a profound need for it. At fourteen I was desperate to "belong." I longed for an extended family and the closeness and security that I fantasized all families had. I felt alone in the world. At that time I couldn't think of another person my age who had no brothers

2

or sisters, who had problems at home, or who wished for someone with whom to wash dishes or walk to school. I needed community, and I found it with 300 other little girls near Hunt, Texas.

I drew strength from the countryside, peace from the river, and a sense of self from the sky. The beginnings of a firm foundation were established in me there. Earth, sky, and river were inexorably intertwined and called me into relationship with them, a relationship that has grown and remained strong today.

We used to sing a song at the riverside. I didn't realize it then, but it was an homage to life; water symbolizes life, for water is a life-giver. The song's lyrics are:

Peace I ask of thee O River;
Peace, peace, peace.
When I learn to live serenely, cares will cease.
From the hills I gather courage
Visions of the days to be.
Strength to lead and faith to follow
All are given unto thee.
Peace I ask of thee O River;
Peace, peace, peace.

Former campers and their families visit Mystic, drive through the gate, stop at the office, and ask to look around, to show their daughters, husbands, or grandchildren where they spent a few summers during their girlhood. They smile and say of some long-ago friend, "She's in Houston now, three boys. Can you imagine?" Or "Poor dear, two divorces! But her daughters still come to camp." Or "Yes, we see her often. She still looks just like she did in Tumble Inn."

They remember, as I do, special memories, memories of those days and quiet nights on the banks of the Guadalupe River, where we were shaped and formed into some semblance of womanhood.

We must be, in part, what we are today because of what we learned in those days at Mystic. Many of us may have a shared experience with those lessons. They are, after all, com-

3

mon values, familiar adages, well-known scriptures, often-whispered prayers. We may have learned the Prayer of Saint Francis at Grandmother's knee. Perhaps we learned the Corinthians "Love Chapter" at Vacation Bible School. Or maybe our parents frequently reminded us, "Be Ye Kind One To Another," as we engaged in yet another rumble with our older sister. Wherever or whoever passed on these words of wisdom did us a great service. They were shaping us into adult, caring, mature humans. They were doing their part to secure us a place in a legacy of common experience.

All of this began for me in the summer, that hazy time of year all youngsters long for. I needed no calendar to count the days. Summer was like the long-awaited visit of a dear friend. I knew the hour of her approach. I waited, in anticipation, with expectation, for her arrival.

Growing up in Fort Worth, I knew it was summer when I began to pack my footlocker for summer camp. One day, usually in mid-March, I would unconsciously begin to rummage through last year's clothes searching for a favorite pair of shorts and a much-loved, soft, and faded T-shirt. Neatly folded and packed away with cut-off blue jeans, a pink tennis outfit (one of those with the little ruffled panties that went under the short, pleated skirt), numerous T-shirts with logos, sayings, and advertisements on them, were my Camp Mystic valuables. Among them: a long string of neatly pinned-together club emblems, a large green felt "M" bordered in gold, three red felt "T"s, and a collection of archery medals. Each year as I unpacked my summer clothes, I came across these hard-won treasures. They were reminders of summers past, of friendships among the deepest I have ever known, of playful days spent by the banks of the Guadalupe River in the Texas Hill Country. They were reminders of my youth, my innocence, my stirrings of spiritual faith, and of the budding of young adulthood.

The medals and felt letters were symbols of achievement, skill, and acceptance. Finding these garments, emblems, medals, and trophies called me to summer. It was time to prepare, to find the list of names and addresses of camp friends, to see who was returning and who was not, to begin to dream

4

and plan for the events and classes that would make up this summer's agenda. It was time to pack my trunk.

Each year I set up my trunk at the end of the hall that divided my parents' bedroom from the guest bedroom. My room was closer to the main part of the house, just across the hall from the main bathroom and a few steps from the den. I wore a path from my room to the guestroom to the place at the end of the hall, collecting necessities and sorting clothes for camp. This was my annual ritual, my rite of spring. Shorts were stacked neatly, T-shirts were folded identically, cotton short/shirt sets were combined and all laid aside. I was methodical in my preparations. One set of cot-sized sheets was collected, along with special pillowcases that had campers' names written on them in indelible ink. According to the list prepared by the camp, I had my Prell shampoo and Tame creme rinse, my Brasivol (a pumice-based facial cleanser I learned about from a camp friend), my Colgate and a new toothbrush, razor and razor blades, Ban de Soleil tanning lotion, a flashlight, a canteen, and a transistor radio. Any other necessities could be purchased from the camp commissary. I was ready. Now I only had five months to wait and I would be at camp.

I did not approach my first summer at camp with such excitement. In fact, I dreaded it. I was an only child and somewhat independent by nature. I made friends easily, but I rarely had many of them, opting for one close friend rather than being part of a "gaggle." So that early-July morning when my mother drove me to the bus station to set me on my way was not one of great joy and expectation.

From my journal, 1964:

> I knew no one. I didn't know any of the cute songs they sang and I didn't understand any of the secret phrases they uttered. "Tonk hill . . . Kiowa Serenade . . . C-C day . . . Guad Squad . . ." Everyone seems a part. They are all "in." I feel out, alone, rejected even before I begin. Each girl has a T or a K on her crisp, white shirt. Most have scores of M's in a long chain pinned together with safety pins. Each M has some sort of symbol on it. None of this makes any sense to me at all.
>
> We stopped along the way to eat the lunches our anx-

ious moms packed for us. (Anxious for us to have a good time, or to see us gone?) I had a sandwich like everyone else, but I DID NOT have the Hostess chocolate cupcake set aside for my sack lunch. My mother's words about gaining weight rang in my ears. I'm 5'4" and 118. Hardly a fatso.

The day was hot. The bus had that kind of canned, electric cool. The a/c blasted and we were comfortable enough, but oh for some real air. The floor of the bus was wet with spilled Coke and Dr. Pepper. Each time you tried to take a step it sounded like your shoes were made of some kind of suction cups. The overhead racks were crammed with stuffed animals, small duffel bags, pillows, photo albums, cassette recorders and the one true essential item ... a GE oscillating fan! The bus is filled with roaring, chanting, singing (if you can call it that) and the bus driver must be going crazy. By the time we passed Austin the singing of camp songs had reached a fevered pitch. Each time we pass some landmark that the girls recognize an even louder roar goes up. I feel like I am on a boat more than a bus. I swear the bus must be swaying side to side as we career down the highway. When will we get there?

After Austin the countryside becomes more distinct—hills, rocky terrain, a kind of warm ruggedness. So this is the Texas Hill Country. We pass the LBJ ranch cut-off. He has been President for almost a year now. I was told that his daughters went to Mystic but since he became President they couldn't return since there was no place for the Secret Service to stay. Soon we pass through Kerrville, then a smaller town, Ingram. Then the Ingram Dam. A loud cheer goes up. All the girls leap to the left side of the bus. Oh God, we're going to turn over. I see the large sloping cement dam ... then behind it Ingram Lake. This is a favorite summer spot I am told. "People slide down the cement dam on their butts," someone tells me laughing. "Some even go down on their feet," she says knowingly. I look at the expanse of the sloping dam and I can't imagine it. I wonder if camp will be as adventurous. The lake, though not large, is large enough to catch the full reflection of sky, clouds, bordering hills and tall cypress, oak, and pecan trees. From this point on to camp we are never out of sight of the Guadalupe River. The river is beautiful ... green ... inviting. It is the friendliest thing I have seen since leaving Ft. Worth some six hours ago.

From Ingram we speed alongside the river past other summer camps . . . Camp Rio Vista, Camp La Junta, Camp Heart of the Hills, Camp Flaming Arrow, and Camp Arrowhead. We have traveled just 10 miles or so and all these camps. We pass through the town of Hunt. A town? It is just a post office, a gas station, and a small run down place called THE Store. The road bends again and we pass Criders, a combination dance hall and outdoor rodeo. Someone chimes in ". . . they serve beer there. And on a clear night you can hear the country western music all the way to Mystic. You can even hear them stomping and dancing." "Wow," I say softly.

The two-lane road ambles on now under a canopy of large trees. Dappled sunlight fills the bus with an eerie feeling, like all of us are under a strobe light. The green-ness of the countryside is dazzling. It isn't lush like the piney woods of East Texas, and it isn't as rugged or majestic as Colorado, but it has a definite kind of beauty. The chaperone is now trying to get us in our seats. She is screaming, "Girls . . . Girls . . . Ladies . . . please sit down . . . we're almost there."

By now everyone is singing, laughing, pointing, screaming, bobbing up and down in their seats . . . all except me. I feel singularly out of place except I am enjoying the view of the land. "I'm so afraid I will be unhappy," I think to myself.

Suddenly a hush comes over the bus. Everyone sits down and begins to crane their necks in the most peculiar way. The only sound is the sucking noise made by shoes moving up and down on the sticky floor, and the whine of the bus engine. Everyone is looking for something. "What are they looking for . . . what does everyone see?' I ask the question out loud because I want to see also. Immediately the girl sitting next to me squeals, "THERE it is." She points to a place high up on top of the hill we are just passing. Spontaneously all the girls begin to point to the same place and they exclaim, some quietly, some at the top of their voices, "THERE it is . . . there is Sky High." I still don't see it and I certainly don't know what Sky High is. "What is it?" I plead. "It's the Mystic sign. Don't you see it?"

Well, it might as well been a holy vision and I still couldn't see it. The sunlight was so fierce that I couldn't see anything outside the bus window, except the river and the looming hills that walled the road. "No, wait a minute," I thought. "I do see something... it's... it's the word M Y S T I C spelled out on top of the hill to our left. So that's it?" I felt pleased that finally I knew what all the commotion was about. Now I had something I could relate to. Just as I was settling in to the idea that I might like this place everyone began pulling belongings out of the overhead racks, from under the seats, and from anywhere anything was stored away. It resembled "abandon ship." No one seemed to care if they were getting their own things, they were just tugging and ripping anything they could get their hands on. And the chaperone began again her pleas of "Girls... girls... ladies..." And to no avail.

From the midst of arms flailing, duffel bags flying through air, and general pandemonium I saw the river at Mystic. It took my breath away. The swimming area, green rafts floating in the water, diving boards, the lifeguard tower. Then, like in a slide show of perfect vacation spots, next slide... a long, green stretch of manicured lawn bordered on one side by the river and a row of stately pecan trees on the other. This green expanse stretched for more than a quarter mile. From somewhere deep inside me I began to move. I too, began to grab for my pillow, my fan, anything I could get my hands on. I may not have been sure about camp, I may have had feelings of regret at being there, but one thing I did know... I was not going to be left behind.

The bus made a sharp left turn throwing us all off balance. Cushioned by our soft duffel bags and heaps of pillows none of us were hurt. We were invincible by this time. Sheer energy and expectation carried us through the next few moments. I remember passing through two rock columns as tall as a man. There was a brass plate that read: CAMP MYSTIC FOR GIRLS. ESTABLISHED 1926.

That was my introduction to Camp Mystic. Shortly after I was escorted to my cabin, Seventh Heaven, I met my first friend, also a first-timer. By dinnertime that night, I was hooked. I loved camp. I loved everything about it; the tribes, the games, the classes, even the heat and mosquitoes and naptime—I loved all of it.

I'm not sure when or why my mother first decided to send me to camp. I am sure, though, that the idea had long been with her. She had been investigating camps and making plans for some time before she announced that I was "going to Mystic." Perhaps she first concocted the idea because I took to Girl Scout camp in such a positive way. Camp Timberlake was a Girl Scout camp not far from Fort Worth. It was a weekend camp, and we slept in canvas tents on cots. There was a latrine out in the woods, and there was a constant scare of bears. I don't know if anyone ever saw bears, or if there even are any bears in North Texas, but we surely heard a lot of stories of them from the older campers and counselors. Each night I tightly tucked in my sheets so that the "bear" couldn't get to me. One night the counselors played a prank on an unsuspecting camper by squishing a banana under the covers near the foot of her bed. When all the lights were out, the sleepy counselor crawled into bed to feel something cold and sticky on her toes. She screamed, and the prankster counselors yelled, "It's the BEAR!" They convinced her that the cold stickiness was the bear licking her toes. I laughed because I knew the truth, but I never felt sure that a real bear might not lick my toes.

Even in those days I was an adept packer. I somehow packed everything I needed for the three-day excursion into one bedroll. That included canteen, flashlight, clothing, swimwear, shoes, brush, Silly Putty, and one Slinky.

Another reason my mother assumed I was good camper material was because of the time I spent with my maternal grandparents on their farm in East Texas near Daingerfield. Every summer from earliest childhood, I went to spend the entire summer with "Momma" and "Daddy." My mother believed it was important for a city-bred girl to have a country experience. Also, since she was a single mother and in the summer I was not in school, it probably facilitated her dealing with the problems of daycare, baby-sitting, and entertaining a precocious and energetic child.

I loved the farm. My grandparents raised polled Hereford cattle on two hundred acres of lush, deep land amid tall pine trees. My two younger cousins lived next door, and they served as the siblings I never had. We rose early, piled into the blue Ford truck with my grandfather, and headed out to the farm some ten miles past town to check on the cows. We knew each one by name. In fact, we were allowed to name any that were born during the summer. There was Bossy (of course), Claudia (named after me by my cousin Bryant), Joyce-a-B (named after my aunt, whose name was Joyce Bryant), and Ladybird (named after President's Lyndon Johnson's wife, Ladybird). After counting heads of cattle and giving them an offering of dried corn on the cob, we set off for town again and my grandfather's Sinclair gas station. Old men sat on the curb, whittling and talking. Their confabulations were punctuated by the occasional "ding" of the bell announcing a customer. My cousins eyed the sodawater tub just inside the station door. It was a large red insulated tub with "Coca-Cola" printed on the front in large, white, script letters. Inside were chunks of melted ice and the coldest water I ever felt. If you were the least bit indecisive about your soda choice, your hands and arms would freeze in no time flat. I liked Grapette. Bryant favored Chocola. Roy Jerdan, the youngest, usually opted for Dr. Pepper. Sometimes we would all get a Coke, then poke a hole in the cap with an ice pick. We could suck those sodas dry. At other times we got a Coke, took the cap off, and poured in a package of salted peanuts. We called that "drink 'n' crunch."

We arrived back at the large white semi-Victorian house by noon sharp, and lunch was served. "Dinner," as we called it in the South, was always accompanied with cooked rice, yellow and thick, made rich with butter and milk. In the summer we usually had blackberry cobbler for dessert. We battled thorns and yellow jackets while gathering the tart, wild berries. After the meal, Momma settled in to shell peas and watch her "stories," or soap operas, on TV, and Daddy took his afternoon nap. I grew up listening to the trials and tribulations of *As the World Turns* and *The Secret Storm*. Why were those characters always crying, I wondered privately, and why was my grandmother so loyal to those programs that she never missed an episode?

I was about as interested in watching "stories" as I was in shelling peas, so I usually wandered through the house. I tiptoed past my napping grandfather in the parlor (who snored so loud and hard the walls seemed to bend in and out with each breath), and by the one bathroom in the house, which had been converted from the original breezeway (all East Texas houses had breezeways in the 1930s and 1940s) when indoor plumbing had been installed. Summoning my courage, I ventured on through the dining room. I say "courage" because the room was always dark and scary. Thick, flowered curtains were drawn, and no sunlight broke in lest "the room fade," as my grandmother said. She was known for being a prankster and trickster, especially to us grandkids, and she would often jump out from behind the dining room door and shout, "BAAAAH," in a deep, moaning voice, with arms held high and fingers spread like claws. I always expected her to rush out and yell as I passed through that room. She put a firm fear of the Boogey Man in us in order to instruct us never to approach dangerous places or suspicious persons. It worked.

On the old screened-in back porch stood the remnants of the water well. The brick well head came up through the wood floor about four feet. There was a wooden cover over the circular opening, and from time to time we were allowed to look down into the dark hole, which seemed to go straight through to the other side of the world. "That's where the Boogey Man lives. Down there with the Devil himself," my grandmother scolded. We believed her, and we were terrified. You could see under the house, because it was built up on brick stilts, and the cats and chickens wandered freely near where the ground met the well chamber. I was certain that the ground would give way someday and suck the chickens down, down into the earth where the Devil himself lived. Of course, that never happened, but I had a deep respect for that scary area under the house and any open well.

Finally, I approached the kitchen, now quiet and still. Food lay out in covered dishes. I sampled leftovers: rice, a bit of remaining steak, a spoonful of cobbler. M-m-m-m . . . nothing better than leftovers.

Unlike my cousins next door, I didn't have to take a nap, so this became a special, private time for me. I whispered secrets to the old bird dog, "Boy," and the orphaned calf we raised on a bucket with a nipple. One time I spent the entire afternoon setting a trap for wild birds in this strange chicken contraption my grandparents kept in the small acreage behind the backyard. It was a coop of sorts, no higher than twelve inches, and it was completely covered with chicken wire. It was about the size of a small cot, two feet by five feet. My grandfather placed older hens in it "to keep them from settin'," he explained. I never figured out if it really worked, or if it was some kind of punishment. "No, no. Bad chicken," I imagined him saying. "Now you will have to go to the short coop."

That day there were no chickens in the "chicken brig," as I called it. Thank goodness. I propped up one end with a brick, to which I had tied a long string, scattered chicken feed on the dirt under the contraption, took my string in hand, and sneaked behind the huge trunk of the nearest pecan tree and waited. There were many failed attempts. Those wild birds flew in for a feast, and as soon as I pulled on the string and the brick tumbled out of the way and the coop fell, the birds flew out and away. Soon, in midafternoon, just before my cousins would be up from their nap, I got lucky.

A large, male cardinal flew in under the coop, along with several sparrows, but he was the prize. I waited, breathless. I watched ever so carefully for any signal that he might fly out. I whispered softly, "Okay, stay there . . . I'm not going to hurt you . . . steady . . . careful . . . NOW!" I gave the string a hearty yank. Birds fluttered. Dust scattered. I jumped up to see if I had caught the beautiful bird. There he was, still under the coop. He jumped up and down, back and forth, frantically searching for an escape hole. I walked around the coop talking to him, trying to console him, but I was cocky, too. I was the conquering hero; he was my spoil of war. Now there was only one problem. How was I going to get him out from under the coop without allowing him to escape?

Gingerly I prepared to lift the coop and cover the angled exit spaces. The cardinal, of course, shot to the opposite end of the coop, far from my arms' reach. I couldn't cut a hole in the chicken wire and just grab him. My trap would be found out. I decided to lie on top of the coop and shoo him to one end. It worked. I slowly rolled to one side and off onto the ground. I was now lying near the exhausted bird. We were almost face to face. Seemingly without effort, I lifted the corner of the coop, reached in, and snatched the bird.

He was the most magnificent thing I had ever held. I carefully cupped my hand around his soft body and raised him to eye level. His head was so perfectly constructed. Every feather was in place, even the little tuft on top of his head. He turned toward me, cocked his head slightly, and seemed to say, "So now what are you going to do with me?" I could feel him breathing beneath my fingers, but he was not trembling. Then I heard the back door of my aunt's house slam shut. I knew THEY were up from their naps and on their way to find me. I couldn't let them see him, because I knew they would want to cage him, and he was far too magnificent for that. Something in me said, "He must be free." So, without saying good-bye, I opened my fingers and he was gone. He flew away so fast I didn't see which direction he went, but he was free, he was a bird again. My grandfather always said, "Wild things should be wild things." This was his explanation for the death of every baby cottontail rabbit he brought us after disturbing their nests during the early-spring mowing. Baby rabbits, box turtles, small squirrels, and all kinds of injured critters were brought to us for pets. Most of them never made it. Many I set free because I believed what he told me.

When I wasn't catching birds, I whiled away the hours of those hot summer afternoons swinging in the tractor-tire swing that hung from a huge pecan tree. The rhythmic pulsing of the cicada's song accompanied me as I lay cradled in the tire, moving gently back and forth, back and forth.

Some afternoons Aunt Joyce made a tea party for my cousins and me. We gathered around the small kid-sized picnic table for Kool-Aid and pecan tassies. Other days we walked to town, up past the Methodist church, on by old Doc Jennings' house and the funeral home that my uncle owned and operated. On the way, we dirtied our hands popping and splatting the bubbles that formed in the soft, tarry blacktop.

Around 4:00 we settled in to watch kid TV at Aunt Joyce's house. Bryant and I scrambled into the same La-Z-Boy rocker and fixed ourselves on the Three Stooges Hour. I'm sure we had seen every episode dozens of times, but that didn't

13

seem to matter. We rocked until the chair nearly jumped off its base or Aunt Joyce called a quick "Quit that!" from the kitchen. Back outside, we played on the "Slip 'N Slide," the swing set, or sometimes just dug in the ground with a large tablespoon given to us by my grandmother. "Here," she said and thrust the spoon with a smile. "Go outside and dig." We did. One time we dug shallow, intertwining trenches all through the backyard. All with that table spoon.

Dusk found us defying the exhaustion that tried to overtake our bodies. Squeezing in a few moments of play before supper, we took turns pushing one another in the tractor-tire swing. Back and forth, again and again, the creaking sound of the chain holding the tire to the tree sang out a monotonous and plaintive song.

My grandparents and I slept in the screened-in porch at the back of the house where it was cool and there was always a breeze. We were bathed in moonlight as we slept. Lying in my bed, I could hear the distant whine of diesel trucks on the highway. The sound of the summer breeze whirred through the woven mesh screen. Sometimes I awoke in the middle of the night and looked out at the phantoms created by evening shadows in Momma's rose garden. I smelled the night air, a mixture of rose blossoms and honeysuckle. It reminded me of summer and my grandmother's perfume.

The memories of those summer days have remained with me in the years since I was a little girl. I continued to return to my grandparents' farm until my grandfather died in 1969, but in 1964 I began to spend only the first half of the summer on the farm. From mid-July to late August, I went to camp. It was as though I had matured past the gentle games played with my cousins. My mother thought it best that I meet other, more refined girls. And she was probably right. I loved my time on the farm. I treasured my summers at Mystic. Summer has always been more than vacation time for me. It has been a time of necessary quiet. It has been a time of growth, both internal and external.

My mother was determined that I was going to be exposed to more than plain fun in the summer. She couldn't afford to send me to a private school during the academic year, but she was sure she could afford to send me to camp. I was not brought up to be a "proper" young lady. I was, however, instructed in manners and politeness. While I am sure not my mother courted the idea of sending me off to a European boarding school, she did consider private colleges such as Stephens, Bennington, and Sophie Newcomb—all places where young ladies could find a "proper education." Camp Mystic was supposed to have been part of that education. She never pushed me to aspire to such things as snatching a good husband, joining one of the celebrated sororities, or becoming a cheerleader. These things may have been in her dreams for me, but they were not in her spoken plans. (I did become aware, however, during the summer after my freshman year of college, that she desperately wanted me to join a sorority, "So you'll have plenty of friends," she said. And that she was an advocate of wearing white gloves to church and to afternoon tea and the wearing of matching underwear at all times).

My mother spent hours calling representatives of particular camps in Texas for information. The first camp I heard her mention was Camp Waldemar, also located near Hunt, Texas. Waldemar was established in the same year as Mystic, and it, too, was a private girls' camp. Waldemar was more expensive than Mystic, and it had a "finishing school" quality about it. As it turned out, Waldemar had a long waiting list, one that encouraged ex-Waldemar campers to enroll their unborn children in hopes of getting them in. Heaven forbid that any should conceive boys!

I later found out that my mother intended to send me to Mystic for one year, place me on the Waldemar waiting list, and hope that I could attend Waldemar in the next few years. Luckily, I never got the chance. Once I was at Mystic, I never wanted to leave.

In those days, the Mystic representative in Fort Worth was a woman named Doris Scott. I never met her, but my mother spoke of her often. It was Doris who gave my mother the name of a current Mystic camper, Marilyn Holmgren. "Call her and ask her about camp," my mother demanded. I was embarrassed to call. I didn't even know her, and I didn't know what questions to ask of someone who was already involved with a place I feared would reject me. I felt silly. But one night, under extreme pressure, I relented and called.

I asked a few polite questions about the cabins, the classes, and the food. I didn't really care about the answers. At that time I didn't really care for Marilyn. Conversation over! It was settled. I was going to camp.

Six pairs of white shorts and six white shirts. I thought we had to wear uniforms. Five pairs of red or blue shorts. Why red or blue? Why not red *and* blue? A canteen, a pillow, a flashlight . . . I checked all the items off the suggested list. These were days before the so-called hippie generation, to whom a less-than-formal look would be acceptable, even desired. Most of the "outfits" in those days of the early 1960s were made of cotton, and they had to be ironed. I decided they also had to be new.

My trunk had come to me by way of my older cousin Johnny. His father was in the air force, and he was well traveled. They had lived in Washington, D.C., in France, and in California. His trunk was one of those old army-style trunks made of thick pasteboard. It had leather straps on each end, two large buckles in the front, and one large snap closure fitted with a key. I renovated it, painted it green, then decoupaged it with newspaper. I must admit it looked quite stylish. Certainly no one would have a trunk like mine. I covered the inside with contact paper, white with raised green daisies. It was not a large trunk, but I managed to fit six weeks' worth of clothes and supplies in quite nicely.

Little did I know this was the beginning of a great adventure, one that would carry me through summers of the 1960s and 1970s. I attended camp for more than sixteen years, both as camper and counselor. In my last two years there, I was the program director. In the years since I left camp I have continued a close relationship with the directors, Dick and Tweety Eastland, and numerous camp friends and associates. Mostly, I have maintained my friendship with Inez Harrison, "Iney" as we called her when she was director.

How was it that this place became so special to me? How did it change my life in so many ways? What forces were at work to shape and mold me into the woman I became? My experience was not singular. Countless women, even generations of women, grew mentally, spiritually, and physically during those summer days along the banks of the Guadalupe River. I am sure any summer camping experience could be a positive factor in a young girl's life. There is something about being outdoors, playing competitive sports, being in relationship with nature in its purest and most pristine form, that not only causes one to look inward, but that asks one to look outward as well, and to make the best of friendships, of conflicts, of personal and professional challenges. But I believe that Mystic offers something more, something even greater than most summer camping experiences. This is, in part, due to the unique blend of courageous role models, in the part of Frank and Inez Harrison, Ag Stacy, Dick and Tweety Eastland, and others who directed and oversaw the program and spiritual thrust of Mystic, and the sheltered environment within which Mystic is staged.

While I was at camp, there was a persistent question that seemed to come up. "Is this the real world? Is this the way things really ought to be? Where people are kind to one another, and sincere, and self-sacrificing? Or is this the unreal place? Is the real world 'out there' beyond the camp gates, where people care about themselves first and foremost, where they will stab you in the back, where material gauges are the only ones that count?" We used to say to one another, "It's so easy to be good here." And it was true. It was easy to be good at Mystic. It became second nature while at camp to turn to prayer when faced with crisis. It became instinctive to think of others' needs and feelings before our own. Why was that? I still don't have a solid answer. Only speculation.

First, it is nearly impossible to be false in such an honest environment. Our true selves are strangely exposed when we are in the presence of nature: clear water, unpolluted skies, an abundance of wild animals living in gentle coexistence with man, and clocked time that moves along with, not in opposition to, natural time. We rose with the sun, crept into our sheltered cabins in the heat of the day, reveled in the cool, crisp waters during the afternoon hours, and, finally, slumbered as the earth did. We moved within nature's time, nature's natural

17

order. We developed an unconscious sensitivity to the rhythms of clouds, of mornings and evenings, for the radiating heat that rose from the earth on sultry August afternoons, and to the occasional sparkles of the natural world: rainbows, fire-flies, meteor showers, and floods. We lived full lives while at camp. We were protected but not immune to either the pains of growing up or the tragedies of the outside world. We were able to keep our youthful innocence intact while we were at Mystic. It seemed like it was the world that had lost its inno-cence and its way. Think about it. Mystic opened before the Great Depression. Girls came. During World War II, Mystic was leased by the United States Army and used for a rehabil-itation camp. Wounded and tired soldiers came to this place to find themselves again. Most found peace of mind, a sense of hope, and their lost faith. A few found wives from the num-bers of young Kerrville girls who used to board buses and travel to Mystic to spend an evening dancing and talking with the soldiers. Then there was Korea, Viet Nam, student unrest, political betrayal, the sexual revolution, the Gulf war, envi-ronmental crises, and on and on. Still, little girls and young women came to capture and re-invest themselves in a personal belief that the world could still be made a better place and that they could make a difference, one person at a time. That was and is our hope: that Mystic can make us better people and, thereby, the world a better place.

Second, the power of Mystic lay in the lives of certain people who dedicated themselves to the spiritual, mental, and physical growth of young women. These were people who looked upon their work as a calling, as a ministry.

Inez and Frank Harrison came to Camp Mystic in 1947 after being wooed there by the owner, Agnes Stacy. They were living in Austin at the time and had met "Ag," as she was called, through Iney's brother and sister-in-law. Frank was hired as business manager and Iney as director. They both ex-celled in their jobs, taking Camp Mystic to unequaled enroll-ments. Soon they were called "Mystic Mom and Pop" by the campers and counselors who grew to adore them. They con-tinued to work at camp until their late eighties.

Iney, though she will approach her ninety-fifth birthday in

18

July 2002, is ageless. Her hair is white now, the color of her eyes has faded, but she looks the same as I first remember her. She works a crowd of parents and campers like an experienced politician. She moves easily through throngs of campers, short and tall, young and adolescent, hugging and offering kisses. In her later years, after the death of her beloved Frank in 1994, she became director emeritus, and she continues to heal homesickness, spread her own special wisdom with her "thought of the day" at Sunday devotionals, and lift spirits with her immutable smile. She lives in Kerrville now but returns to camp each June. On any given summer day you can find her driving "Iney's Ingine" (a customized golf cart) throughout the campgrounds, always accompanied by a high-pitched, whiney chorus of "HighIney . . . HighIney . . . HighIney."

Her face is an expression of love and happiness and reflects a life filled with an optimistic outlook. Ag used to quote Iney's mother, Granny G, who lived at camp during the last years of her life, said that when Iney came to visit, it was like Christmas. And that is true of Iney. She is like Christmas . . . a breath of surprise, a smile, a joyful spirit, and a gift of wisdom.

One time as she walked up Chapel Hill, camp's outdoor chapel, I saw her take off her custom-made gold James Avery earrings to replace them with a pair of papier maché T's and K's made by a camper from Bubble Inn. Iney is like that . . . always willing to take from people who give love and sincerity.

Campers from five decades marvel at her wisdom. To many she embodies the Prayer of Saint Francis; she is patient and kind, faithful and honest, giving and selfless. She knows the secret to a happy life and is willing to share it with anyone who asks in earnest. She is a wellspring of joy and wisdom, laughter and Christian faith. Within the gentle folds of her face is the child Iney, whom none of us had the pleasure of knowing.

During her years as director, she emerged as a unique combination of Dr. Norman Vincent Peale, Maria von Trapp, Thomas Edison, and Mother Theresa. Dr. Peale because of her positive attitude in all situations; Maria von Trapp because of her love for children and her ability to inspire them into practically any accomplishment; Thomas Edison because of her instinctive ability to repair broken toasters, telephones, and padlocks; and Mother Theresa because of her genuine spirit of service to others.

Iney was a savvy businesswoman and a dedicated wife, always putting Camp Mystic and Frank ahead of her own desires. Often she would defer to Frank, allowing him to intervene in a delicate situation when a difficult decision had to be made. They were an exquisite pair; he the behind-the-scenes man, she the outgoing spokesperson for their mutual obsession, Camp Mystic.

The little girls loved and respected Frank, but they saw less of him than of Iney. His focus was the business office and monitoring the boys and young men who worked in the kitchen, at the stables, and on the grounds. Can you imagine being father to more than 600 little girls each summer and having to oversee thirty young men who were well aware of the heavenly circumstances wherein they worked? The boys at camp nicknamed Frank "Eagle-Eye" because he seldom missed anything. Either Iney kept Frank informed or Frank had a window to the world of camp. He had a way of knowing which counselor came in late from her night out, which counselors were involved in raiding the dining hall the night before for ice cream, which young man and which counselor were giving one another the eye, and which camper's parents were getting a divorce. All this he did with the most gentle touch. I never heard him raise his voice, use inappropriate language, demean anyone, or fail to be merciful and give someone a second chance. When I had an administrative position in the office, I had to order Cokes for the Kiowa Serenade, a traditional event in which one tribe of girls "kidnaps" girls of equal age from the other tribe and takes them down to the river for Cokes and Hershey bars after Taps. One day after the order was delivered, Frank asked if I had checked the delivery to make sure it was correct. I hadn't. As I began to offer excuses, he said simply, "Don't ever let that happen again." He wasn't angry, but he was firm. And I never let it happen again. It was a good lesson. Don't make excuses for your mistakes, just correct the problem.

How like a father to instruct, to prepare one for real life, in an understanding and compassionate way. Frank always set high standards for those he worked with, but he never asked anyone to work harder than he was willing to work himself.

Iney and Frank were an ideal pair. Their marriage weathered illness, separation during World War II, and career changes. They continued to work together like a well-oiled machine until the time when, as Iney said, "Frank was called to Heaven."

Dick and Tweety Eastland (her actual name is Willetta, a combination of her grandfather William and her grandmother Henrietta) came to Camp Mystic as a married couple in 1978. Dick, of course, practically grew up at Mystic, since it was his grandmother Ag Stacy and her husband, Pop, who started the camp. At first, the young Eastland thought of it as a vacation getaway at Thanksgiving, Christmas, and Easter. Then, during his early teens, it became a place where father and son grew close. They hunted and fished, and Dick developed a love and appreciation for nature during walks with his father. Now Dick is able to share those same walks through the majestic hills with his own sons. Ironically, Dick and Tweety operate and own a girls' camp, but were blessed with four boys.

Tweety Eastland was never able to come to camp as a camper. Her older sisters packed their bags each summer and headed off to Mystic, but when she was old enough, financial hardships prevented her from attending. Another irony. Now she lives and works at Mystic. It is in her blood.

Dick and Tweety are one of those rare couples who always knew they were meant for each other. They met and fell in love when they were in junior high school. Their interest in one another lasted through the turbulent teens and throughout the college years. They were cheerleaders at the same high school. Tweety recalls, "I sat in front of Dick in English class. We became good friends (I think he liked me because I made chocolate chip cookies even then!). He invited me to spend Easter with his family at Mystic. Dicky took me on a moonlight canoe ride with his dog, Bevo, as chaperone. The smell of the springtime air and the beauty of the stars, the hills, and the trees were all too perfect. I knew I was in love."

Dick and Tweety worked side by side with Iney and Frank

21

until 1991, when Frank and Iney retired and moved to Kerrville. Today Dick is the business manager and Tweety is the director. He teaches fishing classes and referees home plate during the softball games. She dries the tears of homesick campers, makes her famous "Tweety cookies," and serves as role model and idol of every camper there. One day as Tweety and I were talking about camp she said, "You know, this is a ministry. You have to be called to be in camping full-time." And she was right.

Many have been called over the years to devote their summers to the spiritual, mental, and physical growth of young people. There are hundreds, if not thousands, of camps all over the United States. Some specialize in specific activities: tennis camps, riding camps, water sport camps. Others focus on certain themes or directions: religious camps, motivational camps, team building camps. Then still others, such as Camp Mystic, endeavor to make the world a better place. A courageous goal. As Tweety says:

> For hundreds of years the beautiful lands of Camp Mystic served as a real treasure. For the Indians and the early settlers in the Hill Country it was a place of beauty, refuge, and fertile soil. For the soldiers of World War II, it was a place of peacefulness and convalescence. The real treasure, however, is Mystic as a summer camp for girls... Dick and our family realize the importance of safeguarding this treasure, and we want to build on the foundations that Pop and Ag, and Iney and Frank dedicated their lives to. The real treasure comes from watching and experiencing the growth of the campers and counselors during their time here. We watch them leave through the gate knowing that they will be problem-solvers, not problem-makers in the world. We hope and pray that... many lives will be touched in a special way.

While at camp we learned to play tennis, to shoot a rifle, to ride a horse, and to swim. Many of us learned the discipline of making our bed, sweeping and mopping the cabin floor, and generally keeping ourselves and our immediate surroundings clean and tidy. But perhaps more importantly, we learned how to get along with one another, how to share, how to take disappointments, and how to be good friends. Mostly we learned these things by being involved, by doing, and by being exposed to appropriate role models. Many of us came from homes with no sisters, or perhaps no brothers, or as in my case, no siblings at all. Too many of us came from fractured homes. Homes without stability, without support systems, and without traditional role models. Iney and Frank, the counselors, most of whom were college-aged girls, and other campers gave each of us a family. We ate together and talked during the meals about our classes, the weather, whatever was on our minds. There was no television to distract us. There were no newspapers or magazines to interrupt the constant flow of friendly, sometimes frantic conversation. We learned how to live our lives on stable ground, even though it was only for a few short weeks each summer with a group of girls we might not see again for ten months, if at all. Somehow it worked for the majority of us. We learned. We grew. We had disputes and overcame them and still lived happily with one another. We fought bitterly in tribe competitions—the Tonkawas and the Kiowas—but at the end of each game we prayed the Prayer of a Sportsman, we congratulated the winners and praised the efforts of the losers, and then we all found our way to Chapel Hill for some quiet, spiritual time together. Each day was like a year in the ordinary world. We lived entire lives each summer at Mystic.

Now that I am past my camping days and I have no daughters through which I can relive my memories of summers past, I rely on those sharp, treasured glimpses of times there; it might be a word that floats through my memory, it might be a song that serves as a reminder, it might be the smell of summer nights mixed with river sounds. Each day, something calls me back, and I am struck by the realization that I am the woman I am today because of those experiences I had some twenty-five years ago.

Heartfelt is a collection of memorable phrases, values, prayers, and selections from scripture that have stayed with me over the years. From time to time I find myself reciting a verse from scripture, blurting out, "When you get to the end of your rope . . . ," falling back on their inherent wisdom, and searching my memory for an answer at moments of stress or distress. Often I smile when I remember one of the plaques hung over doorways or on the walls of the recreation hall upon which are short, to-the-point admonitions for daily life. One we all used to make fun of was: *I Complained I Had No Shoes Until I Met A Man With No Feet.* We read it out loud to one another as we passed it and cringed. "Eeeuu," we shuddered, "No feet!" But now I often think about that saying. I think about those who may not be as fortunate as others, especially when I am feeling down and wondering if anyone could feel as bad as I do at that moment. Then, out of the blue, I am reminded that there is always someone who is needy and *in need* of our compassion.

This is the manner in which each chapter of this book evolved. I recalled a moment in time from the past as a useful tool for the present. In times of pain, despair, confusion, or loneliness, I have often found myself searching for an answer, an insight, and a direction. Quietly, like a refreshing summer breeze, a memory from camp days gently nudges me, and I am able to find grace, a blessing from something I learned years ago.

I share these thoughts with you. Whether you went to camp or not. Whether you have blissful summer memories or not. Whether you find solace in memories of innocence or not. It is my hope that *Heartfelt* will take you on a journey of faith, of spiritual direction and guidance, and of insight.

Words
to
Live By

CHAPTER 1

It Isn't What Happens to You, but How You Take It That Matters

Just inside the camp office door hangs a plaque made of cedar. It is rustic in design, and its words are burned in and traced in black. IT ISN'T WHAT HAPPENS TO YOU, BUT HOW YOU TAKE IT THAT MATTERS. As a teenager I passed these words a dozen times a week. Years later, when I worked in the Camp Mystic office as program director, I was constantly reminded of these words because the plaque hung over my desk. Today hundreds of girls pass by that plaque and others like it, and I wonder if they notice it, think on it, as I did. Somehow those words find their way into the campers' psyches. Those simple words must emit some kind of magical power, for surely their inherent meaning touches us.

What happens to us in our lives? Good things? Bad things? Things of our own making and things that are done *to* us? Events, moments, episodes, incidents, occurrences, happenings, all in the twinkling of an eye or the flash of an instant. When we tell personal stories we say, "When this happened," or "This happened when I was . . ." We score our lives by the happenings we have lived. We prefer to remember the good times. We can be devastated by the bad times. But how do we react when things happen?

Do we turn to others for help? Do we find ourselves praying? Do we look for direction in appropriate ways? Do we look on the bright side? I hope the answer to these questions is *YES*. We can turn to others for help, insight, support, and guidance. Choose those you turn to with care. We can turn to prayer, not only during the times we feel particularly needy, but also in moments of thanksgiving and joy. We should look in directions that will uplift us and motivate us in positive ways when we seek help. There can be destructive ways to dull the pain or muffle the cries of despair. And we should choose the bright side rather than the gloomy perspective when evaluating events or situations in our lives.

It might sound like a cliché to say, "When life gives you lemons, make lemonade," but that is what really happens when you put your creativity and optimistic outlook to work. It goes deeper than a superficial downplaying of problems as "challenges" and frowns as "smiles turned upside down."

At the heart of making the best of whatever happens to you is a firm belief that you are not alone in the world, that you are not forgotten, that you are not a mistake or a flawed human being. It is important to remind ourselves that we are part of a magnificent creation. This creation has an infinite number of systems and lives to manage and coordinate. Often things don't go as we want or as we had planned. Of course we get upset and discouraged. Of course we lose hope and lash out against whatever or whomever we hold responsible for our plight. But just imagine that you and your circumstances are part of some great plan that you cannot even imagine. It is impossible for us to see tomorrow clearly, because we are in the process of living today. The God who created us and the wondrous world we live in must be in charge. He must be in control of the major events of our lives. Our task is to come to terms with that plan and uphold the best we have to offer, no matter the intricacies of our daily lives.

I had a biology teacher when I was in the eighth grade whom I still remember fondly. He was funny and witty, enthusiastic and challenging. I gained a basic understanding of the human body and its workings in his class, and I still carry much of that knowledge with me today. One thing that I remember most clearly about him was that the last three fingers of his right hand were missing. This slight deformity did not in any way inhibit his teaching. In fact, we found out that those missing fingers were the reason he became a teacher in the first place.

He had wanted to be a medical doctor, an orthopedic surgeon. He was in his second year of medical school when, while on a hunting trip with his father, he accidentally shot off the last three fingers of his right hand. He was left only with thumb and index finger. As he told us the story, he never conveyed any of the physical or emotional pain he must have experienced at the time of the accident. He simply held out his right hand, looked at it, and said, "So I said to myself: What am I gonna do now?" He looked out across the room and smiled. "I figured I could be a stand-up cowboy with a ready-made finger gun," he said and made a clicking sound as he cocked the imaginary trigger, thumb against index finger. "I thought, 'I'll be a teacher, because I have a built-in pointer,'" he said amusingly. Then he pointed with his remaining finger against the blackboard. Everyone in the room swallowed hard. Instinctively, I looked down at my intact hands, palms open. What an impression he made on us in that class. Here was a man with his life ahead of him and BAM, in the blink of an eye he was forced to change direction. Perhaps he could have saved lives with his surgical skills. Perhaps he could have given an injured football player back his game. Perhaps he could have mended all the broken bones in the world. But none of that seemed as important as what he was giving us in that class. We gained from him a respect for the human body as an incredible mechanism. We learned that we were the true wonders of creation. And he did all that with a sense of humor and no anger or regret or misgivings. Maybe he inspired someone in one of his classes to take up the work he had planned to do. I wonder sometimes how many physicians came out of that eighth-grade biology class. Maybe a few. Maybe none. But I do know that he taught us about more than hemoglobin and tendons, muscles and red corpuscles. He taught us about life, and about how sometimes things don't work out as you had planned. He made the best of what could have been a devastating situation. That was a powerful lesson to learn at thirteen.

In the fourth chapter of Deuteronomy, Moses says to the people of Israel, "For ask now of the days that are past, which were before thee, since the day that God created man upon the earth, and *ask* from one side of heaven unto the other, whether there hath been *any such thing* as this great thing *is,* or hath been heard like it?" (KJV, Dt. 4:32) Moses' profound question still speaks to us in today's fast-paced world. Is there anything so wondrous as God's creation of man, and His demonstration of love for that creation? Life is a mystery, but it is a magnificent mystery. Moses questions further, "Did *ever* people hear the voice of God speaking out of the midst of the fire,... and live?... Unto thee it was shown, that thou know that the Lord he *is* God; *there* is none else beside him." (KJV, Dt. 4:33, 36)

We cannot control or predict what happens to us. We can, however, experience all that life has to offer with a grateful heart and a spirit of thanksgiving. Even when tragedy strikes? Yes, even when the unexpected happens, when the most terrible, horrible, and unthinkable happens. In life there are no guarantees, no promises that we will find our way to a bed of roses. Even if we lead good, selfless lives, even if we keep the commandments and love God, we will not necessarily be shielded from harm, pain, or suffering. This can be a difficult lesson to learn. When bad things happen we often become angry... angry at others who might have had a part in our heartache... angry at God because we can't understand why He would have allowed something so dreadful to have happened to us... angry at ourselves because we can't stop blaming something or someone.

In becoming angry, however, we overlook the promise that is part of God's covenant with us. It is a covenant that acknowledges a relationship with us, a bond so strong that nothing can break it. God will be with us, even until the end of time. Jesus Christ manifested that promise and became the incarnation of it. Consider Paul's words to the Romans, "Who shall separate us from the love of Christ? *shall* tribulation, or distress, or persecution, or famine, or nakedness, or peril, or sword?... For I am persuaded, that neither death, nor life, nor angels, nor principalities, nor powers, nor things present, nor things to come, nor height, nor depth, nor any other creature, shall be able to separate us from the love of God, which is in Christ Jesus our Lord." (KJV, Rom. 8:31-39)

One of the most successful books of the 1980s was *When Bad Things Happen To Good People* by Harold S. Kushner. He boldly asks, Why do the righteous suffer? He even goes so far as to ask, "What good, then, is religion," if there are no guarantees of a pain-free life? The staple answer he presents is, *because*. This is not a comfortable answer. It is not a polite or politically correct answer. It is not the answer that many would consider. But it is true. Things, good and bad, happen . . . because. Kushner explains that God does not cause our suffering. In fact, he asserts that God is with us in our suffering. Quoting the Twenty-third Psalm, Kushner offers, "I lift mine eyes to the hills; from where does my help come? My help comes from the Lord, maker of Heaven and earth." (Ps. 121:1-2) He does not say, "My pain comes from the Lord," or "my tragedy comes from the Lord." He says "my *help* comes from the Lord." (Kushner, pp. 29-30) *God* does not cause our suffering. He does not punish our transgressions with suffering. On the contrary, He stands ready to support us in our suffering. He is the "rod and the staff" that comfort us. Our task is to look to Him in times of travail. Our mission in life is to seek Him through the veil of pain that can obscure His love for us and our devotion to Him.

There may be times when it is difficult to find God. In the midst of anxiety or confusion, in the throes of despair or anguish, in times of affliction and loneliness we probe and search for Him. Where is God? Where can He be found? Where is His hiding place? Even Jesus called to God at the moment of His gravest need. His words echo the ancient psalm;

> "MY GOD, my God, why hast thou forsaken me? *why art thou* so far from helping me, *and from* the words of my roaring? O my God, I cry in the daytime, but thou hearest not; and in the night season, and am not silent. But thou *art* holy, O *thou* that inhabitest the praises of Israel. Our fathers trusted in thee: they trusted, and thou didst deliver them. They cried unto thee, and were delivered: they trusted in thee, and were not confounded." (KJV, Ps., 22:1-5)

The prophet Elijah must have asked those same questions as he ran for his life. He begged God to take his life, for he

31

was tired and afraid and completely spent. After receiving food and drink from an angel, he found the strength to travel another forty days and nights until he came to the mountain of God, named Horeb. (KJV, I Kgs. 19:1-9) Elijah thought he was a failure in his ministry. His people, the Israelites, had turned their backs on their covenant with God. They had desecrated the altar of God, and they had slain the prophets of God. Elijah was all alone. He knew that they would try to kill him, too. He was bereft of hope. Then he heard the voice of God telling him to stand on the mountain:

> And, behold, the Lord passed by, and a great and strong wind rent the mountains, and brake it in pieces the rocks before the Lord, *but* the Lord *was* not in the wind; and after the wind an earthquake; *but* the Lord *was* not in the earthquake; And after the earthquake a fire; *but* the Lord *was* not in the fire; and after the fire a still small voice. And it was *so,* when Elijah heard *it,* that he wrapped his face in his mantle, and went out, and stood in the entering in of the cave. And behold, *there came* a voice unto him . . ." (KJV, 1 Kgs. 19:11-13)

Elijah, like us, looked for God in the wrong places. He looked for God in the tremendous, in the gigantic, in the larger-than-life aspects of creation. God is always listening. He is ever-present. But sometimes He is in the "still, small voice." We must find a place to *listen* for Him.

This is something that I first learned at Camp Mystic. God is present, but often in such small and subtle ways that we often overlook *Him*. An older woman who worked in the camp office once said to me, "Be still. Be silent. Be watchful." At first it was difficult to be still and silent. After all, camp is a place of heightened activity and seemingly limitless energy. When there are 300 young girls running, cheering, dancing, and screaming (sometimes all at the same time!) it can seem nearly impossible to find that quiet, private place in which to seek out God. But I trusted those who appeared to have many miles behind them on their spiritual journey. And so I learned, I followed, and I found my way, eventually.

These were gifts first given to me by those who had

learned these things at camp and then lovingly and patiently passed them on to me, often without formal instruction. I learned to discover my faith through watching, observing others as they found their way through tough times, through disappointments, through sadness. I recall Iney saying many times, "The Lord doesn't give you more than you can handle." There have been times when I wondered about that statement. Sometimes I felt like I *was* being given more than I could bear. I discovered, though, that we are, in fact, made stronger through hardship. Not that the hardships make us stronger; rather, it is through learning to cope with hardship that we are strengthened. We learn to walk a well-worn path in times of distress. We become purified like gold in a crucible. And each time we take those steps along that rocky and perilous path, we prove to ourselves that we can find our way to the end of that road. We learn through perseverance that we can find the light at the end of the tunnel. We can learn no other way. It is a personal proving ground. Once disaster strikes, we discover that we know where to go. We are not left alone to our own devices in some black abyss. Through prayer, through supportive friends and relations, through witnessing that others have discovered the same path, we emerge stronger, wiser, and more in charge of our own destinies.

CHAPTER 2

Be Ye Kind, One to Another

Above the main entrance to the camp office is the sign, BE YE KIND, ONE TO ANOTHER. Everyone who passed through the office door saw and read this sign. Sooner or later, everyone had to come to the office... for a phone call, to report a stopped-up toilet, to check in mail, to make an announcement, or to find someone to heal a homesick camper. With repetition, that sign found its way into everyone's minds. I often saw girls silently repeat the words on their way in or out of the passageway. Through silent prayer, or daily ritual, many inscribed those words into their hearts.

Be kind to one another. What a simple instruction! Why, then, does it seem to be so difficult to do this on a daily basis, in the hustle and bustle of daily life? On a given day in any mall parking lot, you can find people threatening and berating one another over a parking space. A parking space, for goodness' sake! There is also evidence of minor crimes and misdemeanors from man toward man on a global scale. Just tune in to any nightly television news program. How are we to have any faith in our fellow man? Why should we trust anyone to be truthful or compassionate or selfless in such an age?

However, there is cause for great hope. The world is becoming a kinder place, despite what the evening news and naysayers proclaim. The following story from an anonymous author illustrates my point:

It was one of the hottest days of the dry season. We had not seen rain in almost a month. The crops were dying. Cows had stopped giving milk. The creeks and streams were long gone back into the earth. It was a dry season that would bankrupt seven area farmers before it was through. Every day my husband and his brothers would go about the arduous process of trying to get water to the fields. Lately this process had involved taking a truck to the local water-rendering plant, filling it up with water, and bringing it back to the dry fields. However, severe rationing had cut everyone off. If we didn't get some rain soon we would loose everything.

It was on this day that I learned the true lesson of kindness and sharing.

I was in the kitchen making lunch when I saw our six-year-old son, Billy, walking toward the woods behind our house. He wasn't walking with the usual carefree abandon of a child, but with a serious purpose. I could only see his back. He obviously was walking with great effort... trying to move as carefully and slowly as possible. Minutes after he disappeared into the woods he came running out again, this time without care. I went back to making sandwiches, thinking whatever his task was, it was now completed. Moments later I again noticed him walking in that slow, purposeful stride towards the woods. This activity went on for an hour. Finally I couldn't take it any longer, so I crept out of the house and followed him on his journey, being very careful not to be seen.

He was cupping both hands in front of him as he walked, being careful not to spill the water he held in them. There could not have been more than two or three tablespoons in his tiny hands. I sneaked close as he went into the woods.

Several large deer loomed in front of him. He walked right up to them. I almost screamed for him to get away, because I could see a large buck with huge antlers dangerously close to him. But the buck didn't move. Billy knelt down, and I saw a tiny fawn lying on the ground, obviously suffering from dehydration and heat exhaustion. The weak creature lifted its head with great effort to lap up the water cupped in Billy's hands. When the water was all gone, Billy jumped up and ran to the house to repeat the life-saving ritual.

As I watched him carry out this act of great and selfless kindness, tears began to roll down my cheeks. I wiped them away but soon more tears ... or was it water wetting my face ... my hands ... the front of my dress? I looked to heaven and saw that it had begun to rain. It was as if God Himself became a part of the healing; healing of the tiny fawn and the land.

For every story of hardheartedness there is an equally powerful tale of someone who went out of their way to soothe, to rescue, to heal, or simply to be present.

Kindness is intertwined with gentleness, compassion, giving, courtesy, mercy, and tenderness. Anyone who practices kindness is also involved in tending others' feelings and thoughts.

At camp I witnessed acts of kindness daily, both subtle and grand. The younger campers, those with the unguarded hearts of true innocence, often felt the impulse to give some token of friendship and appreciation to an older camper or an admired counselor. On lazy afternoons they searched for stones, perfect stones that fit neatly into their petite hands. Once they found these perfect stones, they set out to transform them into works of art, talismans that served as reminders of love, of friendship, of encouragement, and simply to say, "I am thinking of you."

Once I received such a gift. It was from an eight-year-old camper who had a part in the production of *Peter Pan* that I was directing as part of the drama class. She found a small piece of cedar core and carved it into a heart shape, about one inch thick and two inches wide. She sanded it smooth and painted minute daisies around the outside edges. On the center of the heart she painted in tiny letters, "I love you." The gift was a surprise and a delight that I carried with me for many years. Her love for me was born out of innocence, and that inexplicable feeling you have when you are seven or eight years old and you look outside your own family for the first time at someone and say to yourself, "When I grow up I want to be *just* like you." Decades later, when that camper was grown and married, with children of her own, daughters, in fact, and daughters who attended camp, I was able to repay the kindness. On her daughter's birthday, which she was celebrating at camp, I gave her my treasured heart, with a note explaining her mother's kindness to me years before. That painted heart, which smells so softly of cedar and reminds me of walks in the woods, summer rains, and honest friendship, will be passed to others as a symbol of generosity and kindness.

At camp there was a constant exchange between friends of painted rocks, bouquets of random field flowers and grasses, notes of encouragement and solace, and occasionally purchased gifts; books such as *The Velveteen Rabbit, The Little Prince,* any of the miniature books by Joan Walsh Anglund, and collections and anthologies of prayers, memorable phrases, and inspirational verses, such as *Leaves of Gold.* These treasured readings became research centers for any camper needing quotations for a nighttime cabin devotional, Sunday vespers, or letter to a cabin-mate. I first learned about "becoming real" from Margery Williams' Skin Horse in *The Velveteen Rabbit,* a gift from a much-admired counselor. As we gathered around for Friday-night campfires, we discovered the true meaning of selflessness through the ceaseless generosity of the Tree in Shel Silverstein's *The Giving Tree.* I am frequented still by the poster verses of Sister Corita and Joseph Pintauro in *To Believe in God:*

"to believe in God is to get high on love enough to look
   down at your loneliness and forget it forever," or
"to believe in God is to get so attached to everything
   that it can't give up on you," or
"to believe in God is to know that *all* stars are lucky
   ones," or
"to believe in God is to have the great faith that somewhere, someone is not stupid," and my favorite,
"to believe in you is more than I need to make believing
   more than making believe."

Generations of campers became apprentices in the art of making friends by listening to the poignant story of "the taming" from the fox to the Little Prince in Antoine De Saint-Exupery's classic *The Little Prince.* For little girls who were not read to at night, this was our first introduction to the world of great books and remarkable characters.

Today, as I recall the meaning of "Be Ye Kind One To Another," I am struck by the question, "To whom are we to be kind?" We were taught "to one another." But who is *one another*? To our enemies, as commanded by Christ? To our neighbors, as suggested by society? In *Amazing Grace,* Kathleen Norris poses just such a question: "Who is my neighbor?":

> "A man was going down from Jerusalem to Jericho" doesn't seem like much of an answer, but it is the one that Jesus gives. At the end of this story, popularly known as the parable of the Good Samaritan, Jesus allows the lawyer to decide for himself who the neighbor was to the man who had been stripped, robbed, beaten, and left for dead by the side of the road, only to have several respectable people, including a priest, pass him by. (Norris, p. 353)

Samaritans were members of a despised class in ancient Judea. But it was the Samaritan, not the priest or the good Jew, the Levite, who not only saved the poor man, but saw to his care and healing. This is the most well-known and profound example of kindness and compassion in the New Testament. Jesus instructs us to "Go and do likewise." He suggests no restrictions on the instruction. He does not say, "Go, help only those you know, or have common language with, or know to be wealthy and able to repay you, or those whom you know will not harm you later." Jesus simply tells us to be generous and kind and caring to all we may encounter. "Go," and "do," He says.

Kathleen Norris continues:

> It seems clear, from reading the daily news if nothing else, that there will always be some in this world who want their holy wars, who will discriminate, vilify, and even kill in the name of God. They have narrowed down the concept of neighbor to include only those like themselves, in terms of creed, caste, race, sex, or sexual orientation. But there is also much evidence that there are many who know that a neighbor might be anyone at all, and are willing to act on that assumption. (pp. 354-55.)

The Bible is abundant with examples of acts of kindness and of those who act in kind ways. In Matthew, chapter 14, Jesus implores his disciples not to send the throngs who have gathered to hear Him back to their villages: "They need not depart; give ye them to eat." (KJV, Mt. 14:16) Jesus instructs

38

his disciples, and, through them, us, on how to be kind. Jesus does not tell the disciples to gather food and that He will feed them. He gives them the chance to experience this great and miraculous act of giving and sharing for themselves.

Perhaps one of the most moving stories of kindness is found in the New Testament, in Mark, chapter 14:

> And being in Bethany ... there came a woman having an alabaster box of ointment of spikenard [a perfumed oil, often used in burial] very precious; and she brake the box, and poured it on his head. And there were some that had indignation within themselves, and said, Why was this waste of the ointment made? For it might have been sold for more than three hundred pence, and have been given to the poor. And they murmured against her. And Jesus said, Let her alone; why trouble ye her? she hath wrought a good work on me. For ye have the poor with you always, and whensoever ye will ye may do them good: but me ye have not always. She hath done what she could. (KJV, Mk. 14:3-8)

"She hath done what she could." Could any more be said of us? Is there any greater gift that any of us could give? To do what you *can* do, that is a supreme gift in itself. Oftentimes we do nothing, or we do what we *have* to, or we do what we don't want to do. But the unnamed woman in Mark's story of Jesus' anointing in Bethany does what she feels called to do, what she *can* do. For her it becomes an act of lovingkindness. We do not know what happens to her after the anointing. Is she present days later to witness the "anointed one" at His crucifixion? We don't actually know her motivation in bringing expensive perfume for Jesus. Did she believe Him to be the Messiah, and therefore, hope for salvation for herself? Was this an act she had performed before, many times before, perhaps? We don't know these answers, either. We see, quite simply, a woman who went to considerable time, expense, and effort to find Jesus, to enter a dinner party unannounced, and to perform an act of unequaled kindness to Him and for Him. Like so many gospel stories, the act itself opens the way for greater and more meaningful teaching for those not directly involved in the story. Those present (and we do not know exactly who was present at the dinner; it was at Simon the Leper's house, and Judas Iscariot is mentioned in the

Revised Standard Version as being present) are the ones who learn the ultimate lesson: that it is greater to give than to receive, that you must do what you can do, that you must follow your heart, that you must take care of today's responsibilities because you may not be able to do so tomorrow.

When I celebrated my nineteenth birthday, I was a first-year cabin counselor for the youngest campers, ages six and seven, in Twins One. I received dozens of cards from my camp friends, numerous gifts from campers, counselors, and relatives, and I even had a birthday cake, one large enough to feed most of the three hundred plus after lunch. The entire day was filled with "Happy Birthday, Claudia" yelled, called, sung, and chanted. Everyone, it seemed, took part in my festivities.

Late that night, after all the campers were snuggled in their beds, I noticed a lump under my pillow. "Ah," I said to myself with excitement, "another gift." Indeed, it was another gift, but not an ordinary one. Crudely wrapped in a piece of Camp Mystic stationery was a half-used Bic pen. The capped end was wrinkled and dented from chew marks. The ink level was midway down. It was scuffed and scarred as though it had been on the ground. The note, obviously scribbled by one of my six-year-old charges, read, "Happy Birthday, Claudia. I love you. You are my favrit. Love, Flo."

It was clear that the young camper who occupied the bed to the right of mine had stirrings of generosity. She was compelled by the spirit of giving caused by my birthday. She wanted to be a part of it. Like the woman in Mark's gospel, she wanted to do what she could. The size or value of the gift was of no consequence to her, or to me.

As I turned back my bed that night, I looked over at the sleeping child lying almost motionless amid tousled sheets, well-worn Teddy Bear, and pillow. She opened drowsy eyes and whispered, "Did you have a nice birthday?"

"Yes," I murmured. "And thanks," I added with a smile. She snuggled against the bear, pulling the sheets up around her face.

I watched her for a few moments, marveling at her beauty. It was her selflessness I valued. It was the purity of heart I appreciated. A nice birthday, indeed.

CHAPTER 3

When You Get to the End of Your Rope, Tie a Knot and Hang On

Ah! The modern age. More leisure time, more income, more benefits, and more opportunities. And more stress! Never in history have we Americans lived so fruitfully, so prosperously, so successfully. Yet, more of us experience stress, depression, isolation, and disconnection from family, faith, and community than at any other time. Why is this? Why in this age of abundance, equality, and double incomes do we have, on the average, only fifteen minutes of quality time a day with our most intimate companions, our family?

Perhaps this "dis-ease" of the modern age strikes women more acutely, and young women especially. We have been told, if not convinced, that we can have it all. What is "all"? A career, a family, a spiritual life, a community life? And all at the same time? The illusion of "having it all" is that we already have it all, but not to the same degrees and all at the same time. There are always compromises in life. Some things must be put on a different timetable than others. And when our plate is crammed too full, we know it, and so do those who live closest to us.

At one time in our history, young women were satisfied with the prospect of marrying, having children, raising those children, and looking forward to spoiling their grandchildren. The day-to-day routine of running a household, however small, kept most women busy until the evening, and as the old saying goes, "A man may work from sun to sun, but a woman's work is never done." That was true generations ago and is still true today. Now added to running the household and raising the children is the near certainty of work outside the home, traditionally as teacher, nurse, secretary, or shop-keeper. But today women are not limited to those occupations. Mommy may head her own company; she may be a physician, a lawyer, banker, or even an astronaut. The old barriers, we are told, have vanished. Women can be anything they aspire to be. But along with that new freedom and unlimited oppor-tunity comes added responsibility, a growing amount of time spent away from home and a scarcity of personal time.

How can women in the modern age handle more of what our ancestors could barely handle on their own schedules? Of course we have automatic machines to aid us in the labors of washing, baking, heating and cooling our homes, and cleaning. Where would we be without automatic coffeemakers, mi-crowaves, and VCRs? How could we exist in this fast-paced world without cell phones, fax machines, and e-mail? We now have mini-secretaries in the form of handheld electronic plan-ners. We have television sets mounted in our Surburbans, and most youngsters under the age of ten are more computer liter-ate than their teenaged siblings and, certainly, their parents. Where would we be without all these gadgets? How could we live without them and keep up with our constantly changing and ultra-busy lives? The answer is . . . we just might be okay without them!

One of the most important gifts of my summer camping experience was that I learned to simplify, to simplify my be-longings, simplify my schedule, and simplify my life. When my camp friends and I set off for camp, we left behind television, makeup, daily phone calls, overstocked refrigerators, air-conditioning, hair rollers, high-heeled shoes, pantyhose, fin-gernail polish, and fancy underwear. Not to mention ciga-rettes, chocolate, Coca-Cola, alcohol, foul language, mean-spir-ited talk, and late nights away from home. These things, which had seemed so important, were replaced with one oscillating fan, four or five pairs of shorts, five or six T-shirts, one or two pairs of sneakers, a toothbrush, a hairbrush, a bathing suit, and as many pieces of bubble gum as could fit into a small footlocker. We needed only what we could get by with for six weeks of fun, games, tireless play, and the establishment of lifetime friendships.

I don't think we even thought of our favorite television programs once we were settled into our new routine. We never seemed to miss chatting on the phone, though the occasional phone call from home sent us running to the office with chants of "You got a phone call!" echoing from Senior Hill or The Flats. I do confess, however, that in 1969 I missed watching television. It was July 16, 1969, and *Apollo 11* raced toward the moon for the first human landing on that celestial sphere. I was at Camp Mystic, a counselor in Hangout also teaching dance. From my little world in Hangout to those men walking on the moon didn't actually seem that far. From the time the *Saturn V* rocket rumbled its way toward the target, we gazed into the dark, starlit skies to see if we could spot them as they sailed through the blackness. The moonlit skies over camp were magnificent. No lingering light from nearby cities disturbed the immense, clear heavens. A million gems sparkled against the backdrop of black velvet, and the moon hung low in the sky that particular night, looking close enough to touch. I wanted to hear all the reports (even though there was no CNN to give minute-to-minute coverage). I wanted to know the moment the first human foot settled into the lunar dust. No television available at camp, so my camp buddies and I heard about it on the radio. That day at lunch, the entire camp gave fifteen rahs for the astronauts. The volley of rah-rahs felt appropriate. We were safe in our place, and they were safe in theirs. They knew nothing of us, and we knew little of them and their tasks. The moon rose and set over the beautiful water planet, and we went on to our rest hour and the Tonkawa-Kiowa Intermediate kickball game later that afternoon. Somehow the world was at peace that day, and I discovered I didn't have to watch it on TV. I realized that I, like ancestors before me who watched Columbus sail into an unknown and fearsome horizon, or said tearful good-byes to soldier husbands, brothers, and friends, didn't have to experience a video play-by-play to fully appreciate the magnitude of the moment. Little did we know, for most of us had not read Thoreau by the age of twenty, that we were inclined to live, even for only a few weeks, a Thoreau-like life: appreciation of nature, of clouds and sky, of rain and rivers, of one another's smile, and especially a return to the innocence and energy of childhood.

At camp we did not experience the kind of pressure that adults do when making business-breaking deals, managing a full household on a limited budget, or maneuvering 5:00 P.M. traffic on the Katy Freeway in order to make a child's soccer game. Our pressure was less vital to the national economy, yet no less important to a cabin full of eight-year-olds practicing for the junior dodgeball game and rehearsing for that night's cabin stunts, in which they were the star act. Our schedules were tightly fitted to keep us busy, engage us in a variety of activities, such as horseback riding, tennis, water sports, nature studies, archery, dance, chorus, and arts and crafts, to mention only a few, keeping those few who were prone to the affliction of homesickness so active that they hardly had time to think of Mommy and the security of home.

But we did learn distinct life skills that carried us through those packed days and on into our own adult lives. We did learn to "tie a knot and hang on." What was it exactly that we learned to hang on to? What was that mysterious knot we clung to in times we thought we just couldn't make it, or when we were sure we just couldn't go on? Sometimes that knot was made up of one another. The support of friends rallied us to confidence and endurance we didn't know we had, and so we were able to accomplish a goal, win a race, or face a challenge with courage. At still other times, that knot made itself present in role models: counselors, older campers, and especially the camp staff, Inez and Frank Harrison, and Dick and Tweety Eastland.

However, the greatest instruction on stress management became evident in the abiding truth of God's love for us in all circumstances. Time and time again, the adage "When you get to the end of your rope, tie a knot and hang on" was translated into "nothing else really matters when you know that God loves you." We learned that a secure foundation of spiritual faith could carry us through anything. When all seems lost, when no answer appears, when we are left desolate, bereft of hope, desperate and alone, the rediscovery of that simple truth can make all the difference. But that answer often comes in a still, silent voice, a voice that is difficult to discern in a world full of the sounds of technology, babble, environmental clatter, and chaos. Be still. Be silent. Learn to listen for your own still, silent voice and you might find peace, calm, solutions, and direction.

In her book *Simple Abundance,* Sarah Ban Breathnach suggests that inner quiet

> is an authentic awakening, one that resonates with your soul: you already possess all you need to be genuinely happy. The way you reach that awareness is through an inner journey that brings about an emotional, psychological, and spiritual transformation. A deep inner shift in your reality occurs, aligning you with the creative energy of the Universe. Such change is possible when you invite Spirit to open up the eyes of your awareness to the abundance that is already yours. (p. 3)

Can you find time in your busy day to take a deep breath and feel the cleansing power of the warm air as it enters, fills, and leaves your body? Are you willing to locate a special place of your own, fill it with articles that calm you, and spend a few private moments there each day? Are you committed to your spiritual journey to the degree that you make time each day to walk a few steps along that path? Answer "Yes," and profound serenity will accompany you through all the diversions and challenges any day offers you.

There is a crossroads not far from my house that I must pass each time I drive into town. For years I stopped, waited for traffic to pass, admittedly encouraging them in the most impolite language to move faster, then sped on to work, or shopping, or vet, or meeting, or some terribly important function that could not withstand my tardiness. Then one day I came to a full stop, and I sat there . . . no oncoming cars, nothing moving in sight. But I sat there and allowed my mind to wander, to reflect on the bright blue sky, the wispy clouds, the comforting warm air as it filtered in through the open window, and I began to pray. I immediately recalled a friend and spiritual mentor saying to me, "Always come to the Lord first in gratitude." And so I began with a prayer of thanksgiving, "Thank you, Lord, for this beautiful day, for sun and clouds and all that you have given me." Then I prayed for guidance during the day and to be always mindful that it was God's work I was doing and to let Him lead the way. I completed my short prayer with "Thanks again, Lord, for being with me as I cross this road at the beginning of this day." Now, some years later, I have continued to stop and pray at that crossroads each time I pass it. Sometimes my prayer is only a few words: "Lord have mercy, Christ have mercy." Other times I sit for minutes and pray for those in need, for some special intention, or to express gratitude for continued blessings. It has become my prayer road, and it begins the journey of my day and ends it peacefully as I travel home.

At camp we often turned to prayer in times of stress or great need. One time in particular, a young man who worked on the grounds took an evening swim with his co-workers while all the campers were participating in a tribe competitive activity. It was after supper, and as he swam, his body cramped in the cool waters of the Guadalupe. He went under, screaming for help. He knew he was in trouble. In a panic, his friends left the water to call for help. By coincidence, or by heavenly grace, the first people the workers saw was a visiting former camper, now a young woman, and her new husband, who just so happened to be taking a walk along the river at dusk. Another critical coincidence: the former camper's husband had just completed his medical residency. As they rushed to the waterfront, they saw the limp body of the worker being pulled to shore. The new doctor instinctively began CPR with the aid of the head of the waterfront counselor, also trained in water rescue. Together they resuscitated him. In the meantime, the campers had been alerted to some crisis along the river and were naturally curious. Slowly and in calm order, all campers and counselors were led to Chapel Hill, the camp outdoor chapel, where the seriousness of the situation was explained. There the campers and counselors prayed for the life of the young man. They asked God in His wisdom to assist those in the ambulance, the hospital, and those who helped in the initial rescue.

Iney was famous for her praying. We used to joke that she had a "hotline to heaven," but I had never actually witnessed its effects. She was legendary for seemingly instant results from her prayer. One time when her mother, a famous, spiritually wise woman herself, was near death at the age of eighty-eight, Iney called the doctor and then knelt and prayed. By the time the doctor arrived, Granny G, as she was called, was sitting up in bed playing cards. In the scorching heat of many a Texas August, Iney would simply mention out loud, "Lord, we could sure use a rain." And, lo, it would rain. I don't think that Iney was necessarily more spiritual, more wise, or even more devout than most. It was plain though, that she was more focused than most others were. When she prayed, she entered into a different space. Her concentration eliminated all distractions, and it was as though she actually had a "hotline."

That evening on Chapel Hill as we mumbled our separate prayers for the unconscious man, I saw Iney suddenly fall to her knees. Her bony legs landed on the cold, hard rock with a thump. We all heard it and were silent. She closed her eyes, furrowed her brow, and with palms pressed together she said, "Let us pray now for Victor." She led us in a simple prayer, then began the Lord's Prayer. Three hundred little voices spoke those sacred words, and I have never been so moved, or so profoundly aware of the power of prayer. Not because the results were immediate. It would be days before we knew if Victor had escaped permanent injury. No, it was the power of the community experience. We prayed together, and our words melded into one voice directed toward one Creator, who I am certain was listening and returning to us, via the strength of our commitment to the prayer itself, a spirit of calm, reassurance, and serenity. We spoke and we were heard. We were at the ends of our ropes and once again, stillness, quiet, and prayer provided a sturdy knot on which to hang our fears and anxieties.

The Twenty-third Psalm, a scriptural passage used often at camp, provides solace in times of need:

47

The Lord is my shepherd, I shall not want.
He maketh me to lie down in green pastures;
He leadeth me beside the still waters.

He restoreth my soul: He leadeth me in the
paths of righteousness for His name's sake.

Yea, though I walk through the valley of the
shadow of death, I will fear no evil; for thou art
with me; thy rod and thy staff they comfort me.

Thou preparest a table before me in the
presence of mine enemies; thou anointest my
head with oil; my cup runneth over.

Surely goodness and mercy shall follow me
all the days of my life: and I will dwell in the
house of the Lord for ever. (KJV)

King David's sweet song offers us the answer to the question "What do I do when I get to the end of my rope?" The answer is in the simple assurance that the Lord is with us and nothing else matters. Ultimately, we have no want that the Lord will not see us through. We may not receive the answer we would like to hear at the time, but the Lord will be with us through all stress, distress, clamor, and catastrophe. Further evidence is given to us in the final line of the gospel of Saint Matthew: "and, lo, I am with you always, even unto the end of the world." (KJV, Mt. 28:20)

CHAPTER 4

I Complained I Had No Shoes Until I Met a Man Who Had No Feet

A shudder crept down my back each time I passed the sign with those words. Ugh! What a thought! The idea of being deformed or disfigured was bad enough, but to live in poverty was beyond the experience of most of us who attended camp.

We are blessed to live in this country of abundance, affluence, opportunity. Many Americans go to bed with a full belly, wake up to reasonable jobs, and have more things than they have places or uses for. When was the last time you went to bed hungry? Have you ever suffered through an illness because you didn't have insurance or the money to pay the doctor bills? Has your electricity been turned off because you couldn't pay your bill, or have you ever lived without hot water? Without running water? Be happy. You are one of the lucky ones.

A friend shared the following with me:

If you woke up this morning with more health than illness... you are more blessed than the million who will not survive this week.

If you have never experienced the danger of battle, the loneliness of imprisonment, the agony of torture, or the pangs of starvation... you are ahead of 500 million people in the world.

If you can attend a church meeting without fear of harassment, arrest, torture, or death . . . you are more blessed than three billion people in the world.

If you have food in the refrigerator, clothes on your back, a roof overhead, and a place to sleep . . . you are richer than 75 percent of this world.

If you have money in the bank, in your wallet, and spare change in a dish someplace . . . you are among the top 8 percent of the world's wealthiest.

If your parents are still alive and married . . . you are very rare, even in the United States.

If you hold up your head with a smile on your face and are truly thankful . . . you are blessed because the majority can, but most do not.

If you can hold someone's hand, hug them, or even touch them on the shoulder . . . you are blessed because you can offer God's healing touch.

If you can read this . . . you are more blessed than over two billion people in the world who cannot read at all.

HAVE A GOOD DAY, COUNT YOUR BLESSINGS, AND REMIND OTHERS HOW BLESSED WE ALL ARE.

We can all look around and find someone in a worse condition than we are, but it is also seductively easy to look around and find someone better off than we are. Why can't I have what she has? Why has my life not been as blessed as theirs? When will it be my turn? When these questions arise, we fall into the errors of jealousy, envy, greed, selfishness, and self-centeredness. The finale of these attitudes can be hopelessness, depression, and worthlessness.

Little did we know as we passed that sign at camp that it echoed some of the most profound and troubling questions facing Christians in the modern age. Why does God allow bad things to happen? Am I my brother's keeper? How can I feel good about my blessings when many suffer so needlessly? Should I feel guilty when I am relieved that I escaped some tragedy but someone else did not? How can I find God's blessing in everything that happens? Wise men have asked these questions, and so have nine-year-old little girls who have the same capacity for answering them.

Irish scholar John O'Donohue attempts to explain suffering in his book *Eternal Echoes: Exploring Our Yearning to Belong:*

Why is the individual so easily a target of suffering and pain? Why are we so exposed and vulnerable? First, we are vulnerable because each of us is housed in a body. This little clay tent is a sacramental place. The body is in constant conversation with creation; it allows us through our senses to smell the roses, to see the waves and stars, and to read... The body is also very unsheltered... Second, you are vulnerable because you are an individual. To be an individual is to be different. Each individual is separate.... Suffering is suffering because it is an anonymous and destructive force.... Third, we are vulnerable because we live in time. We cannot control time. The tides of time can throw absolutely anything up on the shores of your life.... Fourth, we are vulnerable because of the destiny that is given each of us. Each person who walks through this world is called at some time to carry some weight of pain that assails the world. To help carry some of this pain a little farther for others is a precious calling.... We are all deeply connected with each other. In some strange way, we all belong with each other in the unfolding and articulation of the one human story. Each of us is secretly active in weaving the tapestry of Spirit. (pp. 151–53)

If we think of life as a great and wondrously beautiful tapestry, we see life as complete, neatly ordered, and with no holes or stained portions. Upon closer examination, however, we see a tiny missed stitch, an erroneous double loop, mismatched strands of color, and a coarsely knotted backing. In other words, life may look dandy from a distant view, but look closely and you might see mistakes, problems—the true fabric of living.

Within each life there is pain and joy, suffering and success, hope and despair. No one can truly know what it is to live someone else's life. Some of us are pretty good at masking bad times. Others may, in fact, live charmed lives. One thing is true: no one will be protected from some type of personal hardship or challenge.

Noted Christian writer Paula D'Arcy tells her own story too horrible to imagine in *Gift of the Red Bird:* "as we returned home... our car was struck by a drunken motorist... Sarah died of head injuries... and Roy died three days later... I

51

was twenty-seven years old, three months pregnant, miraculously alive, and shattered beyond any sense. I wished I too had died, and couldn't imagine ever feeling differently. The long journey of grief would consume the agonizing years which followed." (p. 30) D'Arcy goes on to describe the senselessness of it all. She was, in a moment's time, without child, husband, and family. She explains that all she loved was gone and it seemed she was hopelessly at the bottom of a black pit.

From this terrible agony, D'Arcy found her way back to sanity, to life, and to hope. As she recovered, she learned what it was to pray truly. Sometimes you have to pray as though your life depended on it. She states, "I have kicked and screamed at my enormous sense of betrayal by everything I have believed in . . . Being a good person doesn't mean life won't wound you. None of the protections I believed in were real. And now I am left either resenting my life because I didn't get the things I wanted, or learning to love life on its own terms. Really, learning to accept God on his own terms." (p. 33)

How do we accept God on his own terms when those terms are not ones we would choose? How can we truly accept His will? It takes personal courage. It takes faith. It takes courage to trust One who is wiser, One who is in control, One who sees that entire tapestry, not just the close-up version. It also takes faith, but not the great faith we might assume. We are told that faith as small as a mustard seed will move mountains. "For verily I say unto you, If ye have faith as a grain of mustard seed, ye shall say unto this mountain, Remove hence to yonder place; and it shall remove, and nothing shall be impossible unto you." (KVJ, Mt. 17:20)

I confess I have tried that. In an effort to test my faith, or perhaps to prove God's presence, I have prayed to move a mountain. The mountain didn't budge. Does that mean my faith is lacking? Or has God forgotten his promise? Neither, I hope. Although we may attempt to test Him, God does not submit to tests. How many times have we bargained with God, as in, "If you do this for me, I will do ———"? We pledge patience with our little brother, or we promise we won't swear, or cheat, or consume unhealthy substances if God comes through for us. If bargaining were a fair option, we might as well rest content with our old habits, happily assured that God is present and that He forgives us. That isn't exactly how it is supposed to work.

Bargaining with God never works, because we're trying to make the rules. We think we are in charge when, in actuality, it is always the other way around. God is creator of the Universe. He has given us life and the blessed assurance of eternal life through His son, Jesus. We need no more than faith in God's grace to carry us through anything. Faith, after all, is the belief in things unseen. We need no proof that the Shroud of Turin, in fact, has the image of the real Christ in its fabric. We do not need to find the remains of the gopherwood ark to believe in its meaning. Will our faith be increased if the Ark of the Covenant is found after all these years?

Faith is a well that renews itself. It can never be completely emptied. It may be low, at times. We may have to dip deeper and deeper to find refreshment, but with continued perseverance, we can find a way to quench our thirst.

Jesus often spoke in parables, narrative metaphors, which explained simple truths to people who had no formal education; he spoke in symbolic language. A language that had meaning in ways that all people, no matter their age or background, could understand. It works the same for people today, but often we expect the stories to be literally true, exactly as they were written. Many of us have great faith, but the geography of continents has not changed because of the daily movement of mountains. So what did Jesus mean when he said that a small amount of faith could move mountains? The mountain was a metaphor for living life. Could you imagine the creation of the universe with all its diversity . . . creating a sun and moon; night and day . . . humans with all their complexity . . . *and* the great and terrible creations that man has brought about? What is moving a mountain when you consider bringing life into the world, finding a cure for a devastating disease, learning to write and read, or having eternal life through grace? We move mountains every day, but we often fail to realize it because we expect literally to move mountains.

A friend told me of a time when she went to visit her daughter and her two sets of twins. The younger twins had accomplished the tasks of learning to walk and talk. At the time of the visit, they had just completed that last step into self-sufficiency . . . potty training. As my friend got out of her car, the twins, one boy and one girl, ran out to greet her.

The little boy exclaimed, "Grandma, I have panties!" Not to be outdone, the little girl pulled up her dress to expose the newly won prize and yelled, "I have panties, too!"

These two youngsters experienced the realization that they had moved mountains. Think of the enormous effort, knowledge, and perseverance it takes to achieve this level of maturity. We complete some of the most difficult and intricate tasks of an entire lifetime by the age of four. We seldom congratulate ourselves however, because these achievements are expected of us. The ability to speak, to form words based on knowledge of objects, ideas, and perceptions, is probably the most complicated ability we will ever master. That is moving a mountain. But we say to ourselves, "That must be easy. Everyone does it." If we can all do it, it is only because our Creator has gifted us with the greatest of possibilities.

As the childhood story of the *Little Engine That Could* tells us, "I think I can. I think I can." If Jesus were to re-tell the mustard seed parable today, perhaps he would say that if we had the faith of a child, we could move mountains.

When I was at camp and read that sign, "I Complained I Had No Shoes," even though I dreaded contemplating the possibility of having no feet, I was encouraged to think about my fellow man. I often thought about how lucky I was to attend camp, to be healthy and active, and to be able to return to a home that was safe and where I was motivated to aspire to high goals. Not all the campers could say that was true for them. A few were hindered by physical challenges, and a few were even hampered by mental limitations. However, those campers who had difficulties with sports and other physical activities reminded us that obstacles could be overcome, that compensations can and should be made. We learned from one another to count our blessings and not to judge the seeming advantages of others.

If I complain that I have no shoes, I may be so locked up in my own greed or self-centeredness that I may not be open to assisting my fellow man who has no feet. Which is the greater sin? To have so much material wealth that we cannot see beyond it, or to be so weary of our limitations that we cannot see the benefits of a personal challenge?

Ultimately, scripture advises that we not worry:

> Therefore I say unto you, Take no thought for your life, what ye shall eat, or what ye shall drink; nor yet for your body, what ye shall put on. Is not life more that meat, and the body than raiment? Behold the fowls of the air: for they sow not, neither do they reap, nor gather into barns; yet your heavenly Father feedeth them. Are ye not much better than they? Which of you by taking thought can add one cubit unto his stature? And why take ye thought for raiment? Consider the lilies of the field, how they grow; they toil not, neither do they spin: And yet I say unto you, That even Solomon in all his glory was arrayed like one of these. Wherefore, if God so clothe the grass of the field, which today is, and tomorrow is cast into the oven, shall he not much more clothe you, O ye of little faith? Therefore take no thought, saying, What shall we eat? or, What shall we drink? or Wherewithal shall we be clothed? . . . But seek ye first the kingdom of God, and his righteousness; and all these thing shall be added unto you. (KJV, Mt. 6:25-33)

One summer when I worked in the Mystic office as program director, I complained that I never got any mail. "No one ever writes me," I whined. "Poor me," I sighed, keeping the thought to myself. I didn't realize that anyone had heard me, or that they even cared. I was just moaning out loud, looking for something to complain about.

During the remainder of that day, completely without my knowledge, an anonymous counselor went from cabin to cabin to ask each and every camper and counselor to write me a short letter. Sunday was just a few days away, and each Sunday campers had to present a letter before entering the dining hall. Fried chicken was a tradition at camp for Sunday lunch, and campers were encouraged to write at least one letter home a week, so this missive became known as the "chicken letter." The kind counselor suggested that campers write me a chicken letter so that I would have some mail, finally!

When I entered my cabin after lunch on Saturday, my entire cot was covered with piles and stacks of letters, postcards, folded notes, and a few painted rocks. There were more than 350 letters to me, most no more than two or three lines, scribbled, abbreviated with initials instead of proper names, dotted with smiley faces and drawn hearts. There were wishes for a happy day, congratulations for receiving so much mail, sentiments of friendship and love, and most of all, assurance that someone cared for me and wanted me to know that, as evidenced by a thoughtful letter.

I was overcome. Not only had everyone at camp kept it a secret (a task especially difficult for seven-year-olds, who love to whisper a secret), but also the unnamed counselor had been kind enough to pick up on my moaning and follow through with a creative and friendly gesture. I was grateful. I was surprised.

I have kept a box full of those special notes all these years. I review them once a decade or so, usually by accident when I am rummaging through boxes stored in the bottom of a seldom-used closet. Whenever I come across them, I stop whatever I am doing. I sit, read through them, and smile. I see the scrawled name and remember a camper who was eight or ten then, and now I know her to be a wife and mother of three. My heart is warmed. I am reminded of the gift of love, caring, and friendship. How bold we were then to pronounce our love for our friends so freely, to feel no inhibitions in acting sensitively, with kindness and compassion. How wonderful youth can be!

◻ ◻ ◻

Dear Claudia, Camp is fun but hot. You are a great program director and have everything under control!

Your friend, Debby

◻ ◻ ◻

Dear, Claudia How are you. You don't know me but I know you pretty good. I think you are one of the sweetes prosen I know and prettyies too.

Love, Sindy

◻ ◻ ◻

56

Dear Clauida Chicken Letter, It's so much fun here at camp. I love you and love the way you make announcements.

Love, Shannon

□ □ □

Dear Claudia, How are you? How do you feel to talk in front of every single girl of camp? Well I feel good. How many days till camp is over? Well I think I can talk to you later I have to go.

Love, Nicole

□ □ □

Dear Claudia, Hi there! You're probably wondering why I'm writing my "chicken letter" to you. Well, the reason why is I just wanted to let you know that you are doing a fatastic job. I don't know if you realize how much you mean to me and all of us. You're a very special person and a special part of mystic. I don't know how we would get along without you. I love you and I love Mystic.

Love, Joan

□ □ □

Hello Claudia! I just wanted to write you because this term has been great. You helped me because everytime I have seen you you have been smiling. True, everyone gets mad, but you don't take it out on everyone. I admire you for keeping your temper and staying happy and reflecting that on everyone else. Thank you extremely.

All my love in Him, Kanga

□ □ □

Dear Claudia Chicken Letter, Hi! My name is ____ Ha Ha a secret pal! Camp is really fun this year with you around. If we didn't have you we wouldn't know what to do. Well gotta go.

Love, a secret pal.

□ □ □

Claudia, Camp is fun!! This is my chicken letter. I hate chicken but I like you.

Love, Shannon

□ □ □

Dear Claudia, They told us to write you like we write our parants so . . . . . This is our chicken letter! Send money. Ha.

By Allison

◻ ◻ ◻

Claudia, I've known you ever since I can remember! Thanks for always being there when I needed someone to talk to. I hope you stay at Mystic forever. Thanks for being you. We love you and exspecially I love you for your kindness. Your heart is in the right place.

Luv, Lisa

◻ ◻ ◻

Claudia, You don't know me. I go to camp here. They said that you didn't get much mail so I thought I'd write. I adore your long hair. I have long sandy colored hair but not as long as yours. I live in Cuckoo's Nest. I have a great amount of respect for you. You don't ever get angry in the dining hall when we should be listening to you, but instead we are talking. I hope you like us because I know we like you even though we might not always show it. I know God has a special place in His heart just for you. We love you.

Luv, Cyndie

CHAPTER 5

God is First, My Neighbor is Second, and I am Third

Time and time again, campers and counselors have noted that it was easier to be "good" at camp than anywhere else. They felt closer to God and more giving to their campmates. One camper remembers, "I learned so much about friendship, sportsmanship, independence, and myself. I am still learning daily the subtle and indirect things [we were] taught about God and love . . . I can never feel as close to God as I do at Mystic, especially on Chapel Hill." (Sullivan, p. 146)

I have often wondered why it was that it seemed so easy to live by that weatherworn sign at camp, GOD IS FIRST, MY NEIGHBOR IS SECOND . . .

When you live in a place that is surrounded by lovely reminders of God's creation in nature, it is easy to proclaim the majesty of His handiwork. God was primary in our minds as we marveled at sunsets, rain clouds, the clear, green waters of the Guadalupe, deer grazing on newly mowed fields, and even the awesome power of occasional floods and their terrific aftermath. For many of the campers, city girls by birth and upbringing, it was an awakening to have the time and opportunity to watch catfish swim in the deep, cool waters of the diving area, to discover actual prehistoric dinosaur tracks in the flood-washed riverbed, and to *listen* to the tangible sounds of morning or evening.

One camper recalls, "I remember you and those wonderful summer days we spent along the Guadalupe River. You shared many of life's grand secrets with me, right there in the Texas Hill Country.... Your gifts were unconsciously received. You subtly encouraged individual growth and participation in a society of individuals. I wonder if you are conscious of the power and significance of your charm. You are a sentimental time and place, an infinite number of treasured memories." (Sullivan, pp. 6-7)

This camper's memories cloak a young girl's wonder about God. Her reference to "You" speaks of amazement of the natural world around her and her growing curiosity about her place within that world. When we are young, it is often difficult to find proper names for those things that seem too big to understand, so we transfer our love, or devotion, or awe to animals, places, older friends, or heroes we may never have the opportunity to meet.

At camp we were led unconsciously toward a greater understanding of spirit, life, and ourselves. Nature was our guide along this path. Sometimes it is easier to find God, or at least to feel a closeness to God, in the natural world. In times of trouble we often take a walk, sit under the gentle canopy of a tree, or try to work things out in our mind by the shores of a river, stream, or ocean. Why is this? What is it about these settings that put our minds and troubled hearts at rest? I believe we can see our way more clearly when all the trappings of manmade, modern life do not encumber us. Find stillness and quiet, and you will unlock a door to the inner self. It is in the inner self that we find prayer, and prayer is communication with God.

We place God first in our lives when we commune with Him. We are open to discovery of His will, and we can become more in touch with our authentic selves. The discovery of the authentic self *is* the discovery of the God, or divine spirit, within you. When we place God first in our lives, we are, in fact, finding our true path, and thus walking in the way he would have us walk. Whether this path leads us to a specific line of work, or merely a way of living, it enriches the life we live. We become whole, honest, and connected. Connected to those around us, to spirit, and to ourselves. This can be a long and difficult road to traverse, however. Technology and culture lead us in the opposite direction. "Have more. Do more. Be more." These are the watchwords at the dawn of the twenty-first century. We are wrongly advised that you can never be too thin or too rich. "Greed is good," we are told in the film *Wall Street*. And these messages are especially seductive and misleading for women.

In her book *The Road by the River,* Djohariah Toor cautions, "Many places within a woman's soul need healing. In these times especially, human consciousness needs to be open all the way down to the soul level. The feminine spirit itself, an autonomous movement of lifegiving forces within the human psyche, needs recognition and restoration." (p. ix)

Camp Mystic was a place of healing, even though many of us were too young to know we were wounded. Yet, some of us had visible scars. Few of us were untouched by divorce, either directly or by association with a best friend or cabinmate. Death, even violent death, had already touched some by the early teen years. I am sure many were witness to domestic violence, alcoholism, drugs, and gang-related violence either at home or at school. But these misfortunes did not follow us to camp. We left the darkness of the world behind to discover something else, something pure, something unaffected by those mostly urban entanglements, something that could lead us back to that innocent self we had forgotten or misplaced.

As a young girl I found God to be formidable, awesome in power, and I felt that this power could be used in frightening ways. Psychologists might suggest that the masculine role associated with father—stern, unforgiving, strict disciplinarian, often absent—carried over into a youngster's attitude toward heavenly father. This could be true for some, but I lost contact with my biological father at the age of four, so my father was, for me, a fantasy figure. I made up stories based on the scant memories I had of my real father. I recall the time, in the first grade in 1956, that I explained to my teacher that I didn't have a father because he had been killed in World War II. My teacher, of course, was well aware of her American history and basic arithmetic. She quickly added up the numbers and knew

61

I was telling a fib. I don't know even today if I told that lie to protect myself because I felt shame at having no father, or if I was unconsciously trying to make a hero out of an absent and disconnected parent.

Years later, in the eighth grade, when I was involved with a young Methodist group, I remember my eyes brimming with tears and my voice choking with emotion whenever I had to say the name "Jesus." I don't believe I was in a state of mystical grace; rather, I was so unaccustomed to and unfamiliar with the subject of God, prayer, sin, and forgiveness that I couldn't contain my feelings. Camp provided a channel through which these tender and sometimes frightening subjects could be broached. I know that was true for me as well as other young girls finding their way to inner work.

Kathleen Norris confesses, "I take refuge in God's transcendence, continually giving thanks that God's ways are not my own. God has a better imagination." (p. 109)

Some of us discover God through nature, as we have at Camp Mystic. Others find God in family life, through faithful friendships, in journaling or meditation, and in church fellowship. Some who are already well on their journey to knowing God and putting him first in their lives find him in the Word, in sacred writings from scripture, and from writers who focus on the spiritual journey.

One such writer, Macrina Wiederkehr, states, "We are surrounded by the Word of God. It permeates us like the air we breathe. It challenges us to walk with discerning hearts in the company of God ... We are taught ... wisdom through sustained periods of deep reflection and loving attention to the Word ... When you romance the Word, you pursue the Word as it pursues you. You ponder it, pray it, sing it, study it, love it ... Cling to it as to a beloved. Cherish it. Become a home for it." (pp. 11-12)

A good place to begin is the Psalms. The Psalms are poetry that can be used for private devotions. They are reflective, lyrical, thoughtful, energetic, and dynamic. They speak to joy, thanksgiving, sorrow, praise, suffering, and promise, all issues that we face in our prayers or meditations.

Consider these selections:

Psalm 46 . . . "Be still, and know that I *am* God."

Psalm 118 . . . "O Give thanks unto the Lord; for he is good: because his mercy *endureth* for ever."

Psalm 29 . . . "Give unto the Lord, O ye mighty, give unto the Lord glory and strength. Give unto the Lord the glory due unto his name; worship the Lord in the beauty of holiness. The voice of the Lord *is* upon the waters: the God of glory thundereth: the Lord *is* upon many waters. The voice of the Lord *is* powerful; the voice of the Lord *is* full of majesty." (KJV)

In Christian teachings we learn that *relationship* is the key to living a Christian life. This is evident in our relationships with God and with one another. The now-famous acronym WWJD—"What Would Jesus Do?"—reminds us that we should practice the Golden Rule, "Do unto others as you would have them do unto you." In other words, we should practice the relationships Jesus had, with all manner of men and women, in our own lives. But we ask, "Am I my brother's keeper? Who *is* my brother?"

Unlike times past, when most of the people in this country lived in a rural setting, today most of us live in urban environments in which we may not know our neighbors—or even want to know them. We rationalize, "Let someone else take care of them. They can do for themselves. I'm too busy to get involved with my neighbors." We create little boxes for ourselves and shut ourselves inside where we feel safe and secure. We venture out only if we know where we are going and what we may find at our destinations. It takes risk to connect with neighbors. It takes energy—emotional energy and physical stamina—to maintain a connection. But we are taught that caring for our neighbor is the second-greatest commandment. "Jesus said unto him, Thou shalt love the Lord thy God with all thy heart, and with all thy soul, and with all thy mind. This is the first and great commandment. And the second is like unto it, Thou shalt love thy neighbor as thyself. On these two commandments hang all the law and the prophets." (KVJ, Mt. 22:37-40) If we truly place God first in our lives, how can we fail to put our neighbor second?

Jesus interpreted many parables that used the image of neighbor or friend to explain the law of a loving relationship.

Perhaps the most well-known parable is found in Luke, Chapter 10. When a lawyer questions Jesus as to what he should do to obtain eternal life, Jesus replies that he must love the Lord with all his heart and love his neighbor as himself. The lawyer questions Jesus further. "Who is my neighbor?" Jesus tells the story of a man going down to Jerusalem, the story of the Good Samaritan. After telling the parable, Jesus allows the lawyer to decide who had helped the robbed man in the most giving way. The answer from the lips of the lawyer was, "He that showed mercy on him." Jesus instructs us, "Go and do likewise."

This may be the most important thing we can do in the twenty-first century, to consider the question, "Who is my neighbor?" Once we find the answer in our heart of hearts, the next question is logical: "What am I to do for my neighbor?" Charitable contributions make a difference. But simply throwing money at people cannot solve many problems. Not all of us have the extra money to invest in private or civic programs. We must find ways that are meaningful to us to change the world, one project at a time, one person at a time.

We learned this lesson easily at camp. We lived, for five to six weeks, 15 to 25 per cabin. We ate together, all 350 of us. We played together, prayed together, sat together by the river at Friday-night campfires, and rushed the commissary promptly at 3:45 when rest hour was over to get a soda and snack. We learned by doing that the easy way to get along was to do everything together. We had no choice, and it always seemed to work out well. Our communal living taught us the fine art of compromise, whether it was over whose turn it was to mop the floor, or whose cabin was lucky enough to get chocolate cake (the prize for winning that week's cabin inspection) after lunch on Saturdays. The primary object was to accomplish the goal, to get the job done. And if you didn't like the way things worked out, you either suggested a better idea, or compromised and did your part.

One camper recalls:

> During my first year I watched as one of my cabinmates enjoyed a loving friendship with her older sister.... My own little sister and I didn't get along too well in those days.

After being thoroughly impressed with the relationship between [the two sisters] I returned from camp and announced to my sister that we were going to be the best of friends. This announcement had a shaky start but very soon we were actually the best of friends. I am so thankful for that example . . . Thanks to [those sisters] I enjoyed many years of precious friendship that teen sisters often miss." (Sullivan, p. 88)

Another remembers:

My first year at camp I spent more time than I wanted in the infirmary. Several good things occurred during that sickly time for me. I got lots of calls from my mom and dad, visits from my cabin and my older sister's cabin, and best of all, I met a counselor, who while she had several responsibilities, became my friend for the next several years. Each year I looked forward to returning to camp ready to take new classes, meet new people and rekindle old friendships. Mostly, I looked forward to seeing if that counselor was still the same person. And to my relief, she was always there and always the same. While she was older than I was she always took the time to care about me. She was interested in the activities I was taking and encouraged me to do my best. We also talked about friends and family and we took walks together, many times to pick mint by the stream . . . (Sullivan, pp. 98-99)

There was vigorous competition at camp in tribe games, cabin stunts, and cabin cleanup contests. We chanted and cheered until we were hoarse to urge on our team or cabinmates. However, the bond of friendship always was stronger than our individual or team desires. The common goal and "getting along" were the most important things.

There were a few times when a camper just didn't fit in. Homesickness often kept a camper apart from the others, choosing rather to focus on herself and the pain of isolation and separation from where she felt secure. Oftentimes, cabinmates went out of their way to include such a camper, make her feel a part of the activities, and forget her longing. If one was unhappy or uncomfortable, all sensed the tension and set about to correct it. This was the way we learned to put our

65

neighbors first; to let go at times, to listen for an alternate point of view, to sympathize, to understand, and to learn about relationship.

If God is first, and my neighbor is second, then who am I? If I am third, does that mean that I must always be self-sacrificing, always thinking of the other person before myself? How can I justify my needs? How can I feel good about myself if I am continually putting myself last?

In putting God first, we come to know through a relationship with him who we are authentically. In thinking of others, their needs and points of view, we develop a deeper sense of what it is to live in this world. These things being true does not mean that we cannot give attention to ourselves, our needs, our hopes and dreams, our life path, and mostly, our sense of self. All three work together to form a kind of human trinity. God and our relationship with spirit make up one-third of this human trinity. Relationships with others, through which we manifest our relationship with God in human terms, is the second part. And knowledge of and respect for self completes the trinity. We are not whole without all parts.

It is not selfish to pursue one's chosen path. Nor is it self-centered to request others to practice the Golden Rule in their relationships with us. We must have self-respect, courage, self-confidence, and love for ourselves as a creation of God.

One camper lived the teaching "God is first, my neighbor is second . . ." by sharing helpful words with me at a time when I needed uplifting. She took the time to probe my down-trodden spirit and offer me support through this anonymous poem:

> God give me faith in myself. Not only on days when I'm going great and winning and nothing seems impossible . . . but on days when the whole world looks lousy and the road ahead seems too far. When I wonder if I'm brave enough, smart enough, strong enough, and I must be crazy to try.
>
> Don't let me quit, Lord, not ever. Let me keep faith in myself.
>
> No matter how many people discourage me, doubt me, laugh at me, warn me, think me a fool—don't let me listen,

Lord. Let me hear another voice telling me, "You can do it, and you will."

If nobody else in this whole world gives a darn or believes in me, let me believe in myself. I know there will be times when I fail. Lord, don't let my failures throw me. Don't let them weaken my faith. Let them only make it stronger. Let me believe in myself.

I know there will be times when I doubt my own ability, when I'll be discouraged, on the verge of despair. Don't let me give up my faith; hang on to me. Fan the fires of my faith so that I'll try harder. Give me even more faith in myself.

You are the source of life and power and me. You are the source of my abilities—and my faith. Thank you that I can turn to you for reinforcements. That you will give me what I ask—faith in myself.

Iney's Thoughts

CHAPTER 6

The Prayer of Saint Francis

As director of Camp Mystic from 1948 to 1987, Inez Harrison oversaw the camp activities, the hiring of counselor staff, the camper-to-camper and camper-to-counselor relationships, and, most importantly, the spiritual life of the camp. She was an expert at drying the tears of homesick campers; encouraging—no, needling—a camper who had stolen something to "'fess up"; or assisting a counselor with the difficult wording of a parent report on a camper's less-than-ideal behavior. She led us through times of exaltation (the landing on the moon), through sadness (telling a young camper that her father had been killed in an airplane crash), through disappointment (losing the most important tribe game of the term), and through prayer. Iney taught us how to pray.

A counselor recalls:

> I have had several occasions at various religious retreats and weekends to recall the person who, outside my own family, most exemplifies Christ to me, or who most influenced my life. I always think of Inez. I think of her as having a direct line to the Almighty. Too many times I've seen her confront what seemed to be an impossible situation with the words, "Well, we'll just have to pray about it." And before our eyes, God would send the answer, generally by express mail. Iney's faith and love always inspire the best in those

around her. I guess God honors her faith by using those around her as His instruments.

Iney's favorite and most often-repeated prayer was the Prayer of Saint Francis. She read it to us at campfires and Sunday-morning devotionals. She often repeated lines from the prayer, reminding herself of its consoling words:

Lord, make me an instrument of Thy peace;
where there is hatred, let me sow love;
where there is injury, pardon;
where there is doubt, faith;
where there is despair, hope;
where there is darkness, light;
and where there is sadness, joy.

O Divine Master,
grant that I may not so much seek to be consoled, as to console;
to be understood, as to understand;
to be loved, as to love;
for it is in giving that we receive,
it is in pardoning that we are pardoned,
and it is in dying that we are born to eternal life.

Francis of Assisi, who lived during the eleventh century, was born in wealth and died in self-sworn poverty. He spent less than twenty years in Christian ministry, yet his legacy of poverty, devotion, love of nature, and compassion lives on today. He vowed to own nothing in his life, calling on the words from Ecclesiastes, "Lo, this only have I found, that God hath made man upright; but they have sought out many inventions." (KJV, Eccl. 7:29)

Saint Francis, through his life and the prayers attributed to him, taught us to be disciples of Christ. Iney echoed that claim each time she reminded us of his prayer.

There were numerous statues of Saint Francis at camp, usually in quiet places, under a tree, beside a fountain, or near a bed of flowers. Each of these statues portrayed a similar figure with a tender smile, hands cupped at his chest (filled with birdseed), flowing robe, and sandals on his feet. When I was a camper, I never wondered about his poverty, only about his abounding love for little things: birds, deer, squirrels, and children. Unconsciously, I must have connected the words of the prayer with the example set by Iney and the natural beauty of the Hill Country. The tender expressions of that simple prayer have echoed through my mind many times during the past years.

Lord, make me an instrument of Thy peace...

Each of us is called on daily to be a peacemaker; in our families, at work, with friends, in our communities, virtually in every walk of life. Instead of pushing our way on others, we are invited to a place of compromise. Trust yourself and trust one another. Everyone is not out to get you or take advantage of you. Take a moment to see the other person's point of view and work for harmony in relationships instead of discord. "Blessed are the peacemakers," Jesus proclaimed. "They will be called sons of God." We are not peacemakers from a position of weakness; rather, we make peace through strength.

Where there is hatred, let me sow love...

When I first heard this prayer as a young camper, I thought the words were "let me SO love." In my youthful innocence, I interpreted that line to mean, "If someone hates you, so what? Just love them despite their negative feelings toward you." I soon learned that life and, especially, relationships are not that simple. The actual words of the Saint Francis prayer urge us to sow love. Love and a loving attitude can be sown like seeds that, when nurtured, will bring fruit and bounty to all. Hatred is an unweeded garden. It needs tilling. It needs attention and care. Otherwise, the weeds will take over, destroying the beneficial plants. Relationships can be like that, too. If they are not cared for and encouraged to grow in fruitful ways, they become unyielding and of no use to anyone.

Where there is injury, pardon...

How many times have we complained that our feelings were hurt? How many times have we felt victimized by a friend or co-worker who betrayed us in word or action? In how many of these circumstances did we forgive? Perhaps we forgave, reluctantly, but we did not forget. Injury comes in a variety of forms. There is physical injury, injury to one's reputation, the pain of loss of trust, and the injury of spiteful or hurtful words. The pain may be directed at us personally, or it may be the result of someone's insensitivity or oversight of our feelings. Whatever the case, we will all feel pain at the behavior or words of someone close to us at some time in our lives. We can't escape it. However, the pain we feel will remain, fester, and increase if we don't find an appropriate way to release it. We must learn to forgive unless we are willing to live with resentment, bitterness, and unpleasantness. Jesus tells us to "love our enemies," to "turn the other cheek" if we have been struck, but this is difficult wisdom to follow. He reminds us that we should not judge others too harshly. If we complain of sawdust in someone's eye, we may overlook the plank of wood in our own. We must forgive if we are to be forgiven of our own injuries to others.

Where there is doubt, faith . . .

One year at camp I was the drama counselor, and we worked on a production of *Peter Pan*. I recall that summer, and especially that production, as inspired. During rehearsals, we talked of Never-Never Land, fairy dust, and believing that you could fly. Some of the campers in the cast were very young, innocent enough that they still believed in Santa Claus, the Easter Bunny, the Tooth Fairy, and, in certain cases, the Boogey Man under the bed. One night I took a large group of campers out onto the large, green expanse of the golf course to observe the night sky. We located the Big Dipper, the Little Dipper, and the Never-Never Land star. They were amazed. As each girl pointed to the faint star, second to the right of the last star in the Big Dipper handle, they murmured, "Second star to the right, and straight on to morning." They believed, even if only slightly and perhaps for only that summer, in something wonderful, because they could see it. That same evening, we ran the length of the golf course until we were exhausted and breathless, singing, "I Won't Grow Up." We imagined that we could fly. I wanted so desperately to believe that I could fly. Despite our groundedness, we were full of laughter, innocence, and complete hope. We rolled with one another on the cool, damp grass like a litter of rambunctious puppies, until once again we were quiet and focused on the magnificent sky, and that faint star. I began to sing, "There is a place where dreams are born and time is never planned. Just think of lovely things, and your heart will fly on wings forever in Never-Never Land."

In those days it was easy to believe in simple things. We invented the "Gardenia Fairy." There were times when, without provocation, a sweet perfume would fill the air. On one such occasion someone remarked that it smelled like gardenias, hence, the Gardenia Fairy. It seemed that whenever she was detected, something good happened shortly thereafter, and the Gardenia Fairy was proclaimed a good fairy.

Thomas Edison once said that faith "was like believing in things when you were young and didn't know any better." During those long summer days, we had faith, hope, and trust. We modeled our faith after those who practiced their own kind of belief in things seen and unseen. We were young, if not young at heart, and we didn't know any better than to believe what we were told by those we admired and trusted. What better faith education could there be for ones so young and impressionable?

Where there is despair, hope...

Despair is a pit. It is a place so lonely, so out of touch with anything hopeful that it can hardly be reached. It is a place that traps those who find themselves there, believing they can never be rescued. Hope, on the other hand, it the light at the end of the tunnel. It is the assurance that there is still a chance. Hope comes from within when we have discovered that last ounce of strength to carry us on to the next step. It comes from the support of loved ones and even strangers who lend us a helping hand and urge us to go on.

I lived in a time of despair when my marriage failed. I was beyond consolation. I was lost, without hope for the future, seeing no prospect of ever being loved again, and lacking the desire to go on another day. Tears, withdrawal, and depression, and a clock that passed painfully slowly, were my companions.

75

Ultimately, I crawled out from my untimely burial with the help of church, and Iney. I went to Iney because I had no where else to go and, frankly, I was scared. Tears flowed so freely that I didn't wipe them away. She gently pushed the hair from my eyes and prayed for me. She reminded me of Saint Francis' prayer and assured me that I would find hope again.

A few weeks later, at her direction, I returned to church after a long absence. There, I received a dose of reality, and the assurance of God's love and grace for me through the words of Father Michael Boulette, pastor of Notre Dame Catholic Church in Kerrville. "God loves you, Claudia," he told me simply.

"Then how could he let this happen? How could he let me be in such pain?" I cried.

"The promise is not that we will be spared pain. It is that we will never have to go through it alone," he explained. "Even Jesus suffered."

I battled Father Mike during our discussion, trying to find justification for my hurt and my betrayal. I was trying to prove to myself that God didn't love me, or else he would have protected me from this personal tragedy.

Father Mike persevered. "There are many who love you, Claudia. You must return their love and find ways to go outside your pain. Work for others," he suggested. Finally he said, "Your marriage is over, but your life is not. Look for God's blessings in all aspects of your life. Remember, all of life is a blessing if you allow yourself to feel God's grace, in the good times and in the bad." He continued, "Think how God must feel when He loves us so freely and completely, and we do not return that love. God knows the pain of rejection, too."

I had never considered that God was rejected. God feels the same pain we feel? God knows happiness, and sorrow, and loneliness? What a revelation! If Jesus had truly become human, then it seemed only reasonable that He would experience the same human emotions as we do, only perhaps to a greater extent.

Months later, I realized that he was right. Someone asked me why I had returned to church and become so involved in church activities. I replied, "They say there are no atheists in foxholes. Well, I was in a foxhole, and church was the only thing that reached in and grabbed me and held me tenderly." I found my way back to hope and life became full once again.

Where there is darkness, light; and where there is sadness, joy . . .

In 2 Samuel, King David sings his song of praise: "To the faithful your show yourself faithful, to the blameless you show yourself blameless, to the pure you show yourself pure, but to the crooked you show yourself shrewd. You save the humble, . . . You are my lamp, O Lord; the Lord turns my darkness into light. With your help I can advance against a troop; with my God I can scale a wall." (KJV, 2 Sm. 22:26-30)

Darkness into light, despair into hope, sadness into joy. Life is a journey filled with emotion. I recently saw a bumper sticker that read, "Life is a trip. Take notes along the way." If we have faith, if we have hope, we can find our way back full circle to that place where we were full of optimism, full of confidence. Admittedly, we can get stuck in that downward spiral that leads us to despair and hopelessness, but we must continually reassure ourselves that light and joy will return.

O Divine Master, grant that I may not so much seek to be consoled, as to console; to be understood, as to understand; to be loved as to love; . . .

Ups and downs, successes and disappointments are a natural part of any youthful experience. In fact, young people learn to cope with problems they may face later in their lives by testing their patience, endurance, and resiliency in the trials of youth. We discovered through competitive tribe games and through the communal style of cabin life that a loving attitude toward one another led to understanding, and that understanding led us to a compassionate spirit. Time after time, I witnessed a young camper's ability to reach out to another who was lonely and homesick, or failing in some athletic sport. They reached out their hands. They offered kind and supportive words. They waited for them to catch up when the group had run ahead. They offered a smile when someone needed a lift.

A woman who attends my church told me of a homeless man who approached her one day as she was setting up coffee and doughnuts outside the church. He smelled bad and was dirty. He was unshaven, and he shuffled as he walked to the table, eyeing the coffee and sweets. "Can I have a cup of coffee?" he asked shyly.

"Of course," the woman replied. "And have a doughnut, too." His eyes widened as he took the cup of steaming coffee, grabbing an extra doughnut in the process. He began to walk away; then, almost as an afterthought, he turned to the woman and hugged her. She stiffened at the earthy odor of the man, but she did not pull away. He released her and walked away, gulping coffee and chomping doughnuts. "There goes Jesus," thought the woman.

When we do these things for others, we do them for ourselves. Jesus said,

> For I was hungered, and ye gave me meat; I was thirsty and ye gave me drink: I was a stranger, and ye took me in: Naked, and ye clothed me: I was sick, and ye visited me: I was in prison, and ye came unto me. Then shall the righteous answer him saying, Lord, when saw we thee hungered, and fed thee? Or thirsty, and gave thee drink? When saw we thee a stranger, and took thee in? or naked, and clothed thee? And the King shall answer and say unto them, Verily I say unto you, Inasmuch as ye have done it unto one of the least of these my brethren, ye have done it unto me. (KJV, Mt. 25:35-40)

We are the body of Christ, and as such we are instructed to love one another, understand one another, and console one another whenever needed.

For it is in giving that we receive, it is in pardoning that we are pardoned, and it is in dying that we are born to Eternal Life.

When Iney's husband of fifty-two years passed away, she found great solace in the closing lines of this prayer. She lived the words of the prayer by the simple eloquence of her faith. I saw her exemplify the words *pardon, understand, console, love,* and *believe in eternal life.* Frank Harrison was a devout Catholic, and Iney was what we call in the South a "footwashin' Baptist." Their marriage was a monument of trust, compromise, endurance, and loving support. They never had an argument concerning religion. Neither asked the other to change church affiliation. Iney went often with Frank to mass; he seldom attended Baptist service with her. However, their religious and spiritual beliefs were similar. They believed in the promise of eternal life, and they accepted, without question, that Jesus was the Christ and their Lord and Savior. In turn, they both passed these beliefs down to those of us at camp by example. They were excellent, compassionate role models. They have left a lasting legacy in the lives of hundreds of young girls and women.

CHAPTER 7

Amazing Grace

Amazing Grace! how sweet the sound
That saved a wretch like me!
I once was lost but now am found,
Was blind but now I see.

'Twas Grace that taught my heart to fear,
And grace my fears relieved.
How precious did that Grace appear
The hour I first believed!

When we've been there ten thousand years,
Bright shining as the sun,
We've no less days to sing God's praise,
Than when we'd first begun.
—Lyrics by JOHN NEWTON, 1779

There are some melodies that so capture the unconscious that the refrain drifts over us quite suddenly, like a cool breeze on a hot summer afternoon. Out of nowhere and for no apparent reason, the tune finds its way through memory and into sung verse.

"Amazing Grace" is one such song. Sometimes while I am feeding my horses, the hymn pops into my mind. I hum it quietly. I sing a few verses without thinking. It calms the horses, and they stand patiently while I brush their manes or clean their hooves.

I can't remember the first time I heard "Amazing Grace." Its origin is planted so deeply in my childhood that I seem to have always known the words and been comforted by the lilting melody. Today, whenever we sing it at church, tears inevitably fill my eyes. It isn't that it makes me sad; on the contrary, I have the fondest memories of this song, and I have long associated it with Iney. It is her favorite hymn, and we sang it often at vespers services at camp.

One night not too long ago, Iney recalled when she first heard the hymn:

> I was eight years old and we [my family] went to a camp meeting near our home in Friendship, Texas. Tents were set up and there was a great deal of food that everyone had made and brought. We had prayer meetings in the morning, lunch, fellowship time, and in the late afternoon we all went down to the river to be baptized. They sang "Amazing Grace" as I walked into the water to meet Pastor Will Robbins, who also happened to be my uncle. I remember those words "was blind, but now I see . . ." as I went into the cold water and quickly came up for air. My life was changed. That water, those words, that feeling, I knew at that moment that Jesus had saved me and he would be my Savior for the rest of my life. Those were good days in a good Baptist church where everyone knew everyone and prayed and supported everyone. What fun we had!

No matter your church or faith background, "Amazing Grace" seems to have special meaning for anyone who is familiar with it. Kathleen Norris states in her book *Amazing Grace,*

> God loves to looks at us, and loves it when we look back at him. Even when we try to run away from our troubles . . . God will find us, and bless us, even when we feel most alone, unsure if we will survive the night. God will find a way to let us know that he is with us *in this place,* wherever we are, however far we think we've run. And maybe that's the reason we worship—to respond to grace. We praise God not to celebrate our own faith but to give thanks for the faith God has in us. To let ourselves look at God, and let God look back at us. And to laugh, and sing, and be delighted because God has called us his own. (p. 151)

Grace is amazing when you consider that it is freely given, without expectation or without asking. We don't necessarily

have to be good or perfect people; we don't have to be charitable or compassionate. We don't even have to have great
faith. We are blessed with grace because God loves us and because Jesus sacrificed for us, in our name, out of unconditional
love. Amazing! Amazing that I who have infinite capacity for
sin, selfishness, meanspiritedness, greed, even violence
against another should be awarded grace. As the song reminds
us, even a wretch can be saved by grace.

Every camper at Mystic is a member of a tribe: Tonkawa or
Kiowa. The "Tonks" have the buffalo as their symbol, and the
Kiowas are thunderbirds. Through these tribes, campers learn a
healthy competitive spirit, personal discipline through obser-
vance of tribe rules, and a sense of membership, belonging to
something larger than their own scope of being. These are important character-building traits, especially for young girls. Each
Wednesday evening, the Tonks and Kiowas line up at separate
points in the camp. They are waiting for an echoed call to begin
their trek up to their sacred and secret tribe hills . . .

Just as the sun was setting, we heard the faint but clear
call "Tonkawas!" resonate from high on a hill. As we began
our hike up the rocky hill, we were led by the muffled beating
on a tom-tom. No one spoke. As we ascended, the only sound
was hundreds of sneaker-clad feet marching up the slippery in-
cline. Flashlights were almost useless, because we often
needed both hands to brace ourselves to prevent stumbling. By
the time we reached the top of the hill and found our place
around the sacred circle, it was night. The only light was the
campfire that blazed in the center of the circle. Our faces were
lit with the amber glow of the fire. Its warmth was welcome,
even though we were wet with perspiration from the climb.

I often wondered to myself as I sat with my friends
around that fire watching the embers rise, flicker, then fall
away into ash, "How did we ever find our way up here? And
how can 150-plus girls ages seven to seventeen find their way
down safely?" But we did it. Each year we went up tribe hill
and came down again, and usually without injury or a single
lost camper, and all in the near-blackness of a summer night.

We found our way because the path had been laid for us.
Hundreds of campers had walked it all those years before. We

were following the path that others had walked. We were on chartered ground.

I believe that our personal faith journey is like that, too. We go where others have gone before, where they have paid a price—in some cases with their lives, because the journey is sometimes as important as the destination. We don't arrive someday at faith, or maturity, or knowledge. We are continually in the process of becoming.

The hymn points out that "I once was lost, but now I see." We all have been lost at some time in our lives, perhaps actually separated from our parents in a mall or disoriented at a county fair, or after taking a wrong turn on the highway. It is a terrifying feeling to be without course, clear destination, or direction.

At times we become figuratively lost on our spiritual journey, or on the journey of relationship, or we lose personal understanding and awareness. We find our way by seeking the path that others have prepared for us through their experiences. We follow in the footsteps of those we admire, respect, or want to emulate. If we stumble, a helping hand will be there. If we fall back, someone will wait until we catch up. If we lose our way, a direction can be found.

We may have become blind to our direction or life course. Often, we are so absorbed in our predicaments that we become blind to the needs of others, especially those close to us. It sometimes takes a sudden wake-up call to bring us back to our proper course. The hymn supports the idea that grace restores our sight from blindness, either heavenly grace or the grace that comes from personal insight, or supportive relationships.

We must be willing to see the beauty and blessings that surround us each day. Life itself is grace, even though there are times when we would not define it in that way. We cannot experience the pleasure if we do not know the pain. We cannot live surrounded by beauty unless it is shaped and defined by the grotesque.

"'Twas grace that taught my heart to fear . . ."

I have often wondered what it is we fear, or fear most. Studies state that we fear death, flying, being poor or homeless, or speaking in public. Teenagers fear not being accepted by the crowd, or being singled out. Are these really the things we fear most? What about the fear of being separated from God? Or the fear of God not loving me, my own self? What about the fear of not leaving anything of lasting value or permanent consequence after you are gone? It seems to me that these fears are more frightening, and more devastating.

We need not fear being separated from God:

> Who shall separate us from the love of Christ? Shall tribulation, or distress, or persecution, or famine, or nakedness, or peril, or sword? ... For I am persuaded, that neither death, nor life, nor angels, nor principalities, nor powers, nor things present, nor things to come, nor height, nor depth, nor any other creature, shall be able to separate us from the love of God, which is in Christ Jesus our Lord. (KJV, Rom. 8:35-39)

We learn to respect God and his laws through the grace he has bestowed on us. Just as we honor and fear the rules set down by a loving father, we come to know and revere God's prescription for living among one another. This is the grace that teaches us to fear, but it is not the kind of fear inspired by a master with a whip. It is more like an agreement that I have an understanding of the rules and their consequences, and I agree to live under those rules; otherwise, I will face the consequences. We do this readily when confronted by the laws of nature. I know that if the water is deep and I cannot swim, no amount of complaining that I have to get to the other side of the river will alter the rules of nature. If I cannot swim, I will have to find another way across; else I could be in danger of drowning.

If grace (God's ability to demonstrate his love for us) teaches us to fear and honor his laws, it can also relieve us of the fear that God will act capriciously, jealously, or inadvertently. When Moses encounters God in the form of a burning bush that was not consumed by fire, he was very afraid. He was afraid of the unknown and the unknowable. He was afraid for his life. But when he came to know God, though he did not understand him fully, he was able to rely on that fear as a source of faith. Moses experienced grace even though he did not fully comprehend it.

84

"When we've been there ten thousand years ..."

What if we could live to ten thousand years of age? Wouldn't it be wonderful? Or would we become complacent and tired of the same old thing day after day? Perhaps we treasure life so because it is brief.

I have taught theatre and directed plays for more than twenty years, and one of the techniques we stress to young actors is the "illusion of the first time." When you have rehearsed a role for six weeks or more, then performed it four or five times a week for three to six weeks, it is difficult to keep the performance fresh and spontaneous. Actors are encouraged to think of each performance as their first time onstage. After all, it is the first time that audience is seeing the production, and they deserve to see the creative spark shine as bright as possible.

What if we could look at our lives in that same way? Each day is new and original. We will never experience it again in the same way. Each morning that we greet family members is exciting because it welcomes the opportunity for deeper relationship. It is a day added to the tally of time spent together; a precious gift, yet also one day less in a lifetime of allotted days. It is said that no two snowflakes are alike, that no two human fingerprints are identical. The same is true for many moments in our lives.

In Thornton Wilder's play *Our Town,* Emily, a young married woman who has just passed away, is allowed to return to her life for just one day. She says, "I'll choose the day I first knew I loved George!"

Another character cautions her, "No! At least chose an unimportant day. Choose the least important day of your life. It will be important enough." (Act III) Our lives are made of those least-important days, those days we take for granted, and those days we squander.

Each day at camp was important. The days were filled with activities, games, time to share, and time to appreciate nature. Then, at the end of each day, the force of our living and growing was so great that each of us had to rest for a while. Even in our resting we found newness. From the screened windows of each cabin, you could see deer browsing, armadillos rooting, and nightbirds calling. On moonlit nights, the broad shadows of the trees that enveloped our cabins made us feel sheltered, safe, and cradled. The whirring fans blended with the rhythmic breathing of dozens of campers to compose a symphony of innocence. The earth breathed peacefully, storing energy for the next day, which was sure to be filled again with the sounds and sights of the inevitable struggle against time.

We knew that our time for that particular summer was limited, so we lived it to the fullest. We treasured each moment, and we marked the passing of those moments with painted rocks, handwritten notes, rituals of play, and ceremonies of accomplishment. When the end of the session approached, we ached for more time, but time was not ours to control. We wept through the good-byes, parents tearing us from one another's embraces, and we waved good-bye to a time that could not be recaptured, except in memory.

Now, when many of us from those camping days are adults, we savor the memories. Many of us share the experience with our own daughters when they attend camp. Our memories are as precious as when they were first experienced. This can be true of our spiritual journey, as well. That is the message in the song "Amazing Grace": if our days were ten thousand in number, we would recall them all as bright and shining, yet have no less praise for God at the end of our time than at its beginning. Our faith is no less powerful after years of practice than when we first knew God as our creator. We are called to live in wonder at God's creation, never to become indifferent to the variety of life and the experiences it offers. We are called to stand in awe of his wondrous works and his great blessings. We are called to say "yes" to life and to the amazing graces we experience through God and one another.

CHAPTER 8

A Bell Is Not a Bell Until You Ring It

Just inside the camp office hangs a faded black-and-white photograph of a scrawny teenaged girl in striped shorts and a mismatched checkered blouse. She is holding a water pitcher in each hand and smiling coyly at the camera. It is a photograph of Mary Martin, the renowned Broadway star of *Peter Pan* and *The Sound of Music,* when she was a Mystic camper in the 1930s. A letter from Martin to then–camp owner Ag Stacy is attached to the back of the photo, and it reads:

> It was particularly joyous to hear from you about Camp Mystic, too, a place that always has a big spot in my heart. There's a picture of me that was taken there . . . . I do love it because it reminds me of the wonderful times I had at camp and I love it, too, because Oscar Hammerstein has it framed over his desk and he says everytime he looks at it, "I realize there's hope for everyone!"

That photo hung over my desk when I was program director at Mystic years ago, and it always reminded me of how far each of us comes from adolescence to adulthood. I witnessed that every day during my time at Mystic.

Tiny girls stumbled off the bus, wondering where to go and what do to with duffel bag, suitcase, stuffed animal, and all the fears accompanying a youngster in new surroundings.

They enrolled in their classes for the term and went off like sheep, following an older counselor or alumnus to the waterfront, the stables, or the front of Rec Hall. Some couldn't comb their hair, tie their shoes, or make their own beds. A few couldn't remember to spit out their bubble gum when they took a rest-hour nap. I learned quickly that peanut butter rubbed on the gooey-gummed hair relieves the problem as quickly as possible.

By the end of six weeks, these children, some appearing little more than toddlers, learned that their opinions did matter, that they could tie their shoes, wash their own hair, collect their own mail, hit a home run, and accomplish a number of additional feats, and that they were an important and integral part of something bigger in scope than their family, their school, or their home community. In short, they learned personal independence and the beginnings of self-confidence. They learned that they mattered.

The older teenagers exercised their leaderships skills, led organizational meetings, coached a variety of sports activities, and became aware (many for the first time) that they could be valued for something more than looking pretty and behaving submissively.

We confronted ourselves and found something that we liked, even admired. In the company of the feminine, we expressed our genuine femininity. These lessons stayed with us well into adulthood and have shaped lives, families, businesses, and communities for generations.

Mary Martin mentioned Oscar Hammerstein in her photo, and it was Hammerstein who wrote the words that Iney read at the first Sunday devotional for more than fifty years:

A bell is not a bell until you ring it.
A song is not a song until you sing it.
The love in your heart was not put there to stay.
Love is not love till you give it away.

A bell is not a bell, fully exhibiting the clanging characteristics of a bell, until it rings. Then we experience the purity of the sound and know it as a bell. Before that moment, it is only a mass of iron or glass or brass. It has not *become* bell.

Likewise, a song is not a song until you sing it. An unsung song is a collection of notes on a page. If you cannot read musical notes, and even if you can, it is not fully a song until it is heard. Then it is experienced; we are moved or stimulated. We tap our feet, we hum along.

We are not fully human until we express our humanity. As we discover what it is to be fully human, we recognize in ourselves and in others the qualities and traits that give our lives true meaning. Have you ever heard the question "If a tree fell in the forrest, and there was on one there to hear it, would it make a sound?" The answer is no. There must be something to receive the sound in order for it to make sound. Philosopher Maurice Friedman explains:

> Man comes to an awareness of himself as a self not just through his individuality and not just through his differences from others but in dialogue with other selves—in their response to him and in the way they call him into being. Because man lives as a separate self, yet in relation to other persons and to society, present, past, and to come, he needs an image of man to aid him in finding a meaningful way of life, in choosing between conflicting sets of values in realizing his own unique potentialities. Our human existence itself is at once tradition and unexplored future, acceptance and rebellion. The image of man is an embodiment of an attitude and a response. Whether it is an image shared by only one man or by society as a whole, the individual stands in a unique personal relation to it. His image of man is not some objective, universal Saint Francis, but the Saint Francis who emerges from his own meeting with this historical and legendary figure.
>
> The image of man does not mean some fully formed, conscious model of what one should become— ... For each of us it is made up of many images and half-formed images, and it is itself constantly changing and evolving. It proceeds and develops through every type of personal encounter we have: a friend stands by us in a crisis; a poet speaks to us through his poems; a great historical figure affects us through the impact he had on those among whom he lived; the characters of novels and plays seize our imaginations and

enter into our lives through a dialogue we carry on with them in the wordless depths of our being. (pp. 18-19)

At camp our authentic selves became present, in part, because there was no need to display a false one. Twins One, Cuckoo's Nest, or Seventh Heaven, it didn't matter which cabin you lived in—you were accepted, you belonged. We not only borrowed each other's tennis rackets, shorts, or hair rollers, we assumed mannerisms, borrowed clever sayings, and found new ideologies. Like little girls trying on their mothers' high heels and fur coats, we slipped into one another's skin, as it were, saw the world from a different point of view.

A bell is not a bell until it rings; faith is not faith until it is tested. Courage is not courage until it is challenged, and love is not love until it is shared.

I confronted the depth of my own courage on a stormy night in August 1978. I was program director, and one of my most pleasant duties was to check cabins after everyone was in bed, making sure there were two counselors in each cabin and that everyone was settled—no homesick campers crying, no hair caught in the electric fan, no giggle-fits in the bathroom. It had been raining hard that night, and we feared flooding. I had been through numerous floods in the past and, although they could make a mess, for the most part, the awesome power of the water was exciting to watch. This time I knew it was different. Counselors were returning from their night out with tales of low-water crossings covered with a foot of water or more. I could see for myself that water covered the Cypress Creek crossing and was lapping at the steps of Senior Hill.

Under normal conditions, Cypress Creek was less than a foot deep at the crossing that separated Senior Hill from the remainder of the camp. Junior campers often fished at its banks, and all could observe bass nesting in its shallow, clear waters. That night it swelled out of its banks and surged over the road. A great cypress tree stood at the base of Senior Hill a few feet from the creek that shared its name. A flood light with a painted green hood was attached some ten feet up on the trunk of that tree.

All through the night, the campers on Senior Hill, and

those of us in the office, kept sight of that light as a marker of the rising waters. In the early hours of the morning, it became a vigil light holding our hope and our courage.

The summer of 1978 had been particularly hot and dry. The morning hours in June were usually pleasant—cool enough, in fact, for a sweatshirt. The campers in beginning swimming at 9:15 A.M. shook and trembled at the thought of learning the basics of the American Crawl and the backstroke, not because of fear but because of the icy cold water, which transformed their suntanned bodies into blue-tinged, goose-bumpy, giggling mermaid forms. But this June was different. By 10:00 A.M. it was near eighty. By noon it was ninety-five. At 3:00 P.M., as rest hour was ending, it approached one hundred degrees, or more. We dreaded August.

By August we had rearranged the camp schedule. Instead of riding classes in the afternoon, there was a free swim for everyone. There were times when, after breakfast, we let everyone go back to bed for a "rest morning," just so that they could replenish their strength and energy. The nurses encouraged us to take salt tablets at lunch, and we drank pitchers full of water, iced tea, anything wet.

Often, in the hour just before evening, a group of counselors and campers circled the flagpole for a rain dance. Part serious, part in good humor, we usually began with a prayer. Whether we were praying to God or to the "god of Guadalupe rain" was not clear. However, our chants and stomping and our offerings of flower petals were performed in earnest. We needed a break from the heat, and we needed rain!

There was little relief at night. The friendly whirring of the fans sounded more like the roar from a furnace. Bed sheets stuck to throbbing legs and sweaty torsos, and the hot air sank onto pillows and teddy bears.

Occasionally a cloud passed by, momentarily shrouding the scalding sun. Spontaneous crowds would gather round the flagpole for the by-then famous rain dance. Our lanky shadows mirrored the dance, but the sky burned cloudless.

The real pleasure of those sizzling days was a shower. Once just part of the daily routine, a shower became an indulgent ritual. No need for hot water; we took the coldest showers possible. Where once we languished under a stream of steamy hot water, now each of us waited for that icy film to pour over sticky limbs, washing over wilted faces and finding its way to every part of our bodies. It was a baptism that brought relief from the summer sun.

August 5 again brought in a blazing ball. Clear—no forecast of rain. The day dragged forward. Cicadas screamed. Noon. Not a blade of grass moved. The air was still sucking the energy out of anything that dared to move or breathe. Afternoon. Walking across the Flats felt like moving in an incinerator. Evening. Dinner was intolerable. Three hundred and fifty in one large dining room felt more like a thousand. All seemed to inhale and exhale at the same moment, and the touch of someone's sticky arm against yours was cause for a riot.

Then, suddenly, something unexpected happened. At first I thought someone had brushed my side. I turned to see who it was, and to tell them to "get away." But no one had passed me. The dinnertime chatter subsided for a second. Apparently others had the same sensation. A moment passed. Then another. Again, quite suddenly, I had the same feeling, only this time it felt friendly. Again, the roar of laughter, talk, and singing ceased.

It was then that I realized what had happened. A feeling of delight filled the dining hall. It was a cool wind that had selected a camper here, or a counselor there, brushed by them, flitted to another, and then, like a friendly phantom, escaped unseen. Sprite-like, impish, as though it was alive, it came again. It moved over the tables, disturbing wisps of hair and dropping napkins to the floor, as elusive as Tinkerbell and twice as mischievous. We laughed, not knowing why we suddenly felt giddy. Then, from the tables nearest the east side of the dining hall, campers rose from their chairs, straining to see outside. Quickly, others followed. Pretty soon we were all standing, looking to the east as though waiting for the first sunrise. The word "rain" dashed about the hall. "Will it? Is it? When is it?" The anticipation was palatable. But rain did not come that evening.

Our disappointment was overcome by the fact that it was cooler and breezy. We finished cabin stunts, reported to cabins at 9:30 P.M., and heard Taps at 9:45. All was quiet, relaxed, and still. But in the far, far distance, a low rumbling was heard. It sneaked in secretly, moaning and crying. It was thunder.

Our prayers were answered, finally. The rain began around 11:30 P.M. At first it was a slow, steady rain, then it began to pour. Great sheets of rain fell, limiting visibility to only a few inches. Then the bellowing thunder came, volley after volley, shaking cabins, beds, and campers, rolling and echoing throughout the canyons.

The lightning lit everything in sight like a black-and-white slide show. A brightly lit image . . . darkness, another image . . . then blackness again. Lightning strikes were coming every few seconds, always followed by a thundering crash, BOOM! The wind blew ferociously, sweeping sheets of rain into every open window. For the first time that summer I was cold, chilled to the bone by the wind and rain.

The rain was coming down so hard by now that it was difficult to see familiar landmarks: the flagpole, Iney and Frank's house (called "Pop Inn"), Rec Hall, and Heaven Can Wait (the infirmary). Soon we received calls from ranches upriver forecasting the river's rise and the speed of the rise. The boys who worked on the grounds and those of us who were in the office scrambled down to the river to move waterfront equipment to safer ground. Canoes, diving boards, metal chairs, fishing equipment, paddles, snorkel gear, Styrofoam floats, everything had to be moved, and quickly. I scarcely noticed that when we first began moving the canoes, the water lapped around my ankles. By the time we loaded the paddles and pads, we were wading in hip-deep water. It was time to leave the waterfront. Our clothes were soaked, so it felt much colder than the 70-degree temperature. I shivered as I ran back to the office for the next report on the water level.

By now the Guadalupe River and Cypress Creek were a raging torrent of whitewater and tumbling tree trunks, moving with a deafening roar. Someone came running into the office to report strange sounds coming from under the oldest senior cabin, Hangover. Hangover got its name because it hung over the side of Senior Hill. It was braced with eight huge wooden poles cemented into the side of the bluff. The sound we heard that night was that of loose logs and other debris hitting those braced poles. We feared that Hangover's foundation might be weakened. I did something then that had never been done before. I turned on the PA system and spoke carefully into the microphone in the middle of the night. My announcement must have blared throughout the camp mixing strangely with the sound of the howling river, now completely out of control. "Attention Senior Hill . . . campers in Hangover, please move now to Rough House [the nearest cabin with its foundation securely on flat ground]. Don't worry, we're okay here on the Flats, just please move as quickly as possible to Rough House." We could see the lights come on in all the seven cabins on the hill. Then, dozens of voices called in unison from the hill, words that settled our fears: "Claudia, is the river awake yet??!"

Each Sunday morning at devotionals I had pointed out that the river "was asleep" because in the early-morning hours it was glassy and smooth. The day's winds had not yet picked up, causing gentle ripples to disturb its surface. The senior campers remembered my allusion and pointed out that the river certainly was awake now.

Moments later, Nancy, a first-year counselor living in Bug House, the last cabin in a line on the Flats, came into the office and announced breathlessly, "Claudia, the water is over the big rock next to Bug. What do we do?" Stacy, who worked in the office and was Nancy's sister, entered the office at that moment. She looked at me, rolled her eyes, and for a second I thought we would both laugh out loud. We both knew Nancy was prone to exaggeration.

"Now, Nancy, are you sure?" I questioned, not believing that her answer could be yes.

The line of cabins on the Flats faced the Guadalupe River but were seventy-five yards or so from it, nestled at the base of the mountain we called "Sky High." In addition, there was a steep berm that lay halfway from the river to the cabins. Nonetheless, Nancy was sure that the river had expanded so much that it now threatened the cabins.

"Over the rock?" I said, my voice squeaking.

"Yes, *over* the rock," Nancy stood fast to her answer. "I tried to keep the kids quiet, but they could see the water with their flashlights, and they're scared."

I just couldn't believe it. I had witnessed numerous floods, and the water had never approached Bug House or the barrel-sized rock near its base.

"Now, Nancy," I said calmly, "You know the water has never been that high. I want you to go back and check it. Then come back and tell me where the water is."

As she turned to go, I grabbed Stacy and told her to accompany Nancy. "Find out how high the water really is."

The two were off into the silvery night. I watched them as far as I could as they jumped puddles and skirted lightning flashes, until they were shadowy silhouettes against the blinking sky.

Fifteen minutes went by, and in the meantime I contemplated what to do if the reports of high water were indeed true. "My God," I thought, "we'll have to move every camper on the Flats to higher ground. That's almost two hundred campers!" I shuddered from the cold and the fear of what might lay ahead. I searched for dry, warm clothes and quickly changed out of my soaking shorts and T-shirt. I armed myself with anticipation, a pair of dry cut-off jeans, and an old football jersey that I hadn't worn in years.

Meantime, I looked again toward Senior Hill. I could see, in the reflection of the green floodlight, water rushing by and growing closer to the light source. Then the light appeared to go underwater, and instantly it was black. Somehow, at that moment, I knew we were in for real trouble. For the first time I considered that we were in danger.

Stacy and Nancy returned to the office out of breath and wide-eyed. Stacy said flatly, "Claudia, the water is up to the big rock." Nancy nodded, implying, "See, I told you so."

"Okay, we'll have to wake up Iney and Frank and start moving campers. Try not to alarm them. Tell them it's precautionary." I paused and added, "And tell them it's a great adventure."

I looked at my watch. It was 2:45 A.M. "What a time to wake up Iney and Frank," I thought. Stacy and I grabbed hands and ran toward Pop Inn. "It's gooonnaa fllloooooood!" we exclaimed, half gleefully, half frightened.

No sooner had we knocked on the door that it opened. "Oh, girl. It's gonna flood," Iney said. "Get in here." She already had spoken to the people upriver (at World's End Ranch, no less) and knew that the water was coming down at an alarming rate. "There's gonna be a wall of water coming down soon. You all be careful," she cautioned.

We told her that the waterfront chairs and canoes were secured, and that the water was coming over the big rock at Bug House.

Closing her hands in a prayerful motion she quickly said, "Well, that's it. We've got to move all those campers to Rec Hall. Let's get to it."

The next hour was a blur. We awakened sleeping campers, quickly explaining that we were moving to Rec Hall and answering questions such as: "Does this mean it's flooding at home in Houston, too? . . . Can I take my Teddy Bear? . . . What about my sister on Senior Hill? . . . How long will we be in Rec Hall? . . . Should I pack my trunk before we go?" One camper had all her belongings on her cot, including trunk and duffel bag, and was planning to sail away when the waters came.

By the time all were safe in Rec Hall, I was exhausted, shaken, and shivering. I stood with Stacy in the dark, listening to the roaring river in the distance, and realized what we were experiencing. "Stacy," I said trying to reassure myself under the guise of explanation, "I'm not scared. I'm just cold and tired."

The thunder and lightning had subsided finally, but the rain continued in a downpour. I could see that the flagpole was surrounded by water and the road to the counselor parking lot was completely flooded. I looked toward Senior Hill. The steps were underwater. I turned off my flashlight, resigned to the fact that we were completely cut off from Senior Hill. Then Stacy touched my arm.

"Claudia, the water is coming into Casa Rio. The girls are flooded out."

Casa Rio was the area below the dining hall. It housed the

kitchen staff in dormitory-like apartments. The water had never gotten that high. Now we wondered if the dining hall itself was safe.

The hours rushed by as fast as the water rose. We surveyed the rising water from the porch of the dining hall. It was clearly past the huge pecan tree that sheltered us during devotionals and campfires. The pecan tree was at least fifty feet from the edge of the waterfront, but now it stood like a lone post in a sea of churning logs, distorted house parts, and broken limbs.

There was little else we could do except watch, and wait, and pray. Senior Hill and the Flats were secure, and the Casa Rio girls were safe, though all their belongings were, by now, soggy and ruined.

By 5:00 A.M. the rain stopped. The sky was clear and blue and the air was clear and cool, like after a spring shower. If you focused on the hills you might never have known what the night before had brought. But the evidence was clear everywhere else you looked. Huge cypress trees were uprooted along the river. The standing cypress trees were scarred and peeled twenty feet up. The once-lush waterfront was buried under eighteen inches of silt, slime, flopping fish, and debris. The Cypress Creek crossing was still underwater, though the depth was now only about two feet. It no longer raged and rushed. It seemed almost peaceful. It was still too dangerous for the campers on the hill to attempt to cross to get to the dining hall for breakfast. A few of us mounted horses, playing female knights, and carried plastic bags filled with cartons of milk, jars of peanut butter, loaves of sliced bread, and plastic knives and forks to the stranded campers. Breakfast that morning would be served in bed and from horseback.

Those of us in the office began to consider some of the real problems at hand. Luckily, we never lost phone service, but the water was not safe for drinking until it could be tested. Parents had to be notified, somehow, that we were all safe, information which radio and televised news reports were neglecting to impart. Some people had drowned far downriver, and the damage was catastrophic.

The water level at Hunt was calculated at seventeen feet

above flood stage. In Kerrville, some twenty miles downriver, it was twenty-one feet. Medina, Bandera, and Comfort had suffered the most—thirty-four feet of floodwater.

Two counselors' cars were taken downriver by the force of the water. Another car from the highway ended up nose-down in the Guadalupe. Tons of rock from up in the canyon was now dispersed in the Cypress Creek bed. The golf course was hidden under a thick layer of brown, slimy silt, the green Bermuda grass smothered. The golf box was nowhere to be seen. We joked that it was probably downriver to the next camp by now. "Maybe they could use it," we joked.

Surveying the damage, I realized how truly powerless we humans are in the face of nature and its awesome power. The river had taken on a different personality. For so long we had thought of it as languid, peaceful, and lovely, and as a friend. We had taken her for granted. Within the life of all rivers is the possibility of rage, an unrestrained force that devastates all within its path. We had witnessed the full power of the Guadalupe, and we would never look at nature or the river in quite the same way again.

After the flood, we worked to help clean up the damage. We scooped buckets of silt from the waterfront and golf course. We removed downed limbs and righted waterfront chairs and canoes. We struggled to put our home back together. But we were changed by that experience. We survived, but also we matured. We grew into a closer, yet more wary relationship with nature—water, sky, wind, and rain.

We could tell our grandchildren about this! Gratefully, no one had been injured; in fact, most campers thought it was exciting, even fun. Parents had T-shirts made that read, "I survived the Flood of '78" and sent them to their daughters. A news helicopter landed on the waterfront to get the latest report, and a National Guard helicopter landed to see if we needed any medical supplies. Further excitement. More stories for our grandchildren.

Soon, it was time for Intermediate Softball on the diamond in front of the infirmary. We cheered, laughed, screamed at the home run, and gathered afterward for prayer on Chapel

Hill. Life was back to normal. The flood was a memory by now . . . at least until the next sound of thunder.

The test of courage had found us in different places, some in their cabins, others in positions of authority, still others in internal and private places. Because of the flood experience and the group work in its aftermath, we discovered an unknown side of ourselves. In subtle ways, we would never be afraid in quite the same way again. And that new strength and courageous spirit would linger in the hearts of many of those campers and counselors for their entire lives.

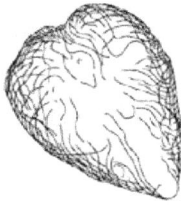

Prayers
and
Scriptures

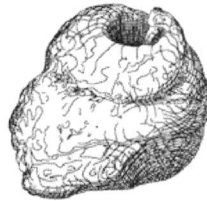

CHAPTER 9

Psalm 121

I will lift up mine eyes to the hills,
from whence cometh my help.
My help cometh from the Lord, which made heaven and earth.
He will not suffer thy foot to be moved:
He that keepeth thee will not slumber.
Behold, he that keepeth Israel shall neither slumber nor sleep.
The Lord is thy keeper:
The Lord is thy shade upon thy right hand.
The sun shall not smite thee by day, nor the moon by night.
The Lord shall preserve thee from all evil:
he shall preserve thy soul.
The Lord shall preserve thy going out and thy coming in
From this time forth, and even for evermore.

This hymn to God expresses confidence and trust in the ultimate power of his love and attention to us, his people. The original writer of these words no doubt looked up to the hills, toward the heavens and the illuminated sky, and found there his God. Although this psalm was written more than two thousand years ago, we can relate to that young man who gazed upward in praise, in thanksgiving, in need, and in triumph.

Our bodies and our labors are confined to the earth. Our dreams, hopes, prayers and spiritual selves, however, are not. It is instinctive in us to "look up" to God. That aspect of ourselves that is not limited by time, or space, or physical restrictions exists in another realm, a place up and out there. Certainly God lives in our hearts, too, but when we seek him, when we are in need of his grace or assurance, we often look to heaven. It is as though we locate God first by finding him in sky and space, beyond the stars and brighter than the sun; then, once we feel in communion with him, we call him into our hearts and minds. It is at that point that we become spiritually connected to the divine, in prayer or in meditation.

We are assured in Psalm 121 that God is creator of the universe. He made heaven and earth and all creatures that inhabit it. It is also apparent in this psalm that God loves his creation, man, enough to guard him and protect him from all harm.

The psalms are divided into types. There are hymns of praise, such as Psalm 33; "Rejoice in the Lord, O ye righteous: for praise is comely for the upright." There are laments, such as Psalm 61: "Hear my cry, O God; attend unto my prayer. From the end of the earth will I cry unto thee, when my heart is overwhelmed: lead me to the rock that is higher than I."

There are hyms of thanksgiving, such as Psalm 121, and royal psalms, such as Psalm 110: "The Lord said unto my Lord, Sit thou at my right hand, until I make thine enemies thy footstool." And there are wisdom psalms, such as Psalm 112: "Praise ye the lord. Blessed is the man that feareth the Lord, that delighteth greatly in his commandments."

Each type of psalm has a different tone, mood, and purpose.

Psalm 121 is a psalm of thanksgiving, but it is personal in style and voice. This is not a psalm of a nation or great army giving thanks. It is the song of a simple man who has found confidence in his God and is proclaiming his prayer openly.

God is presented in this psalm as vigilant. Unlike man, who may tire or become restless or bored, God is always in control. He is beyond human needs. He will not sleep or walk away or tire of caring for his human creations. It is interesting that the psalmist refers to "thy" instead of my, as in the case of Psalm 23, "The Lord is *my* shepherd." It is as though this psalmist, perhaps King David, has discovered his personal faith and is now projecting that assurance outward to others. He says, in essence, "God will not forsake you. He is your keeper and he protects you."

104

It is important to remember that the psalms were written long ago and in a language that uneducated people could understand and find meaningful. Those ancient people, however, were not ignorant. In fact, they probably were better versed in the scriptural texts, through spoken exchange, than are most of us today. They easily interpreted the symbolic language to meet their needs. For example, the ancient Hebrews did not expect to be protected from the heat of the sun. They lived in an arid and temperate zone. Heat, sun, and scorched earth were a fact of life for them. They probably interpreted "The sun shall not smite thee by day, nor the moon by night," (KJV, Ps. 121:6) as "You have nothing to fear; God will protect you from harm. You do not even need to be afraid of the darkness." Furthermore, the psalm tells us that if you follow God and his commandments, you will be protected from all evil of the earth. Again we hear God's promise, one which is proclaimed in the Old Testament and echoed in the New Testament, especially in the writings of Saint Paul.

We are mortal creatures. We cannot be protected from suffering, even death. However, the promise is that we will never be alone in our suffering. We are loved, and we will be welcomed into God's holy kingdom during this life and in the next. The psalmist declares that the Lord is present at our coming in and our going out: our coming into the world and our leaving it, as well as our daily coming and going. We are never separated from God and his lovingkindness. The psalmist believes this to be true for himself and for us, too.

Beautiful hills surrounded us at camp. During the summer they were covered with green foliage on live-oak, mountain cedar (better known a juniper outside of Texas), Spanish oak, and other varieties called scrub oak, pin oak, and hackberry. The trees on the lowlands near the rivers or creeks were pecan, sycamore, and bald cypress. The valley on which Mystic was settled was like an open palm. We were held safely there, and I often imagined that the waterfront and adjoining open area were like the palm of God's hand.

From the waterfront, you looked across the river and the highway that ran parallel to it to a large bluff we called "Billy

Goat Bluff" because Spanish goats often walked up and down its ledges as nimbly as though they were on flat ground. The bluff was bare of trees and scrub brush except at its base and some thirty feet up where cedar and mountain laurel struggled, stunted, through solid limestone. On clear summer evenings, the bluff reflected the sun's dying glow from off the shimmering waters of the Guadalupe. For about an hour each evening, the bluff was a screen of changing color from light pink to dusty rose at sunset, then a gold-tinged magenta, until finally, the blue darkness of night enveloped the bluff, the waterfront, everything except the sparkling river. On full-moon nights, the river became a crystal mirror upon which fireflies and other night creatures of the air danced with their reflections. Frogs, turtles, and snakes swam, dove, and cavorted in the cool black waters. (I learned how to tell if it was a snake or turtle swimming in the water by the shape of the wake around its head: a turtle makes a round shape, and a snake makes a V shape.) Nutria (beaver-like rats that are quite good swimmers) and occasionally an armadillo traversed the width of the Guadalupe, the nutria on the surface and the armadillo, believe it or not, steadily walking along the bottom from one side to the other.

Campers who awakened during the pre-reveille, early-morning hours watched deer graze peacefully in the dew-laden grass. The morning birds' happy songs mingled oddly with boom-box tunes blaring from cabins. Girls laughed and squealed on their way to breakfast. All the world, it seemed, was awake and prepared for a new day. Fresh-faced girls met the bright warm sun, and who could tell which was the more beautiful?

Beyond the camp's main compound—the cabins, office, dining hall, and infirmary—lay an additional 700 acres. This land was used mostly as grazing area for the horses, riding trails, hiking and overnight camping sites. It was a wonderland of assorted wildlife: white-tail deer, gray and black squirrels, possums, raccoons, skunks, armadillos, wild boars (javelinas), blackbuck antelope, moufalon sheep, axis deer, and, sighted on a few occasions, a panther, a mountain lion, and a Mexican black bear.

This part of camp, which most of us rode, hiked, or wandered through, was ideal Hill Country land. The rolling hills fell into deep canyons, where streams gathered and wildlife settled in the evening hours. Huge bluffs overlooked meadows of wildflowers that resembled colorful quilts spread out for some grand picnic. This land was left untouched. No roads, no buildings of any type (except for the occasional deer blind used during hunting season in early winter), no scar of man's intrusion. The land was a mystery to us city girls. It could be foreboding and achingly beautiful. It spoke of loneliness when the summer's winds whirled dust devils and shook the trees until they appeared like shivering old women dressed in long capes.

The rustic quality of the land prompted ghost stories and romantic fantasies. There was the story of "Dead Man's Gulch," which frightened many unsuspecting campers to the point of tears when it was passed on from one who, just the year before, had heard it and cried. Hormone-driven teenagers lay outside tanning under the sun, silently, with strange smiles on their faces. They dreamily imagined being carried off into the hills by some Adonis on horseback who planned to take them to his palace and smother them with hot kisses and promises of life-long love.

One spot in particular was Chamber-of-Commerce, picture-postcard beautiful. It was called Natural Fountains. At a deep curve in Cypress Creek, shrouded by cypress and sycamore trees, was a carved-out bluff. We used to imagine that the ecru-colored limestone was actually coffee ice cream and God had scooped his finger through the side of the bluff for a taste. That's what it looked like, as though some great giant, or God, had run a finger along the inside of the bluff, and what remained was a hollowed-out formation. Sometimes we sought shelter from sudden summer storms in this cavern. The floor of the bluff was wide enough that we could ride horses along the inside shelf. The topside of Natural Fountains flattened out onto a large, rocky pasture dotted with cedar and pin oak trees. We called the ledge that overlooked Natural Fountains "God's Mountain."

At one point, the bluff remained hollow, but two tower-like structures rose from the creek bed almost to fifteen feet, where a gentle cascade of dripping water met the top of each tower. Long ago someone had installed a bucket at the top of each to catch the water. Over the years, layers of limestone had encased the buckets so that they were no longer visible. The entire structure appeared completely natural. Each tower was covered with dense green moss and maidenhair fern. There were no steps up to the water; years of campers climbing their way to the top had formed slight footholds and indentations that aided future climbers. There was only enough room for one person at a time to slide and claw their way to the top, but once having made it to the summit, the rewards were a drink of clear, mountain-filtered water and a feeling of having climbed Mount Everest. We dropped our heads, facing skyward, to allow the fountain to drench our faces, necks, hair, and clothing. We giggled as the water trickled down our shirts or swimsuits. We cupped our hands, catching enough water to throw down to the next camper, splashing her head and making her more eager for her ascent to the throne.

Those campers who still believed in Santa Claus, the Easter Bunny, and the Tooth Fairy (the Tooth Fairy visited often at camp) thought that God lived at Natural Fountains. Sometimes they were sure they heard him walking through the brush on the opposite side of the creek. The older campers chided them, saying, "Oh, come on! It was only a deer running through the thicket." But maybe the proverbial "mouths of babes" were correct. Maybe God did reside in that lovely spot. Where else should He be?

Natural Fountains was sacred: sacred to animals who called it a safe and bountiful home, sacred to campers who discovered, many for their first time in their lives, the sacredness of place.

For many campers and counselors, past and present, Mystic has become a sacred place. It is a shrine to all that is possible. Love, friendship, harmony—all these were experienced at camp. We became attuned with nature, its order and inherent wildness. We discovered ourselves and the possibility of what we could become. Most importantly, our summers at

Mystic taught us to search out the holy, and to return to that sense as often as possible.

In his book *The Re-Enchantment of Everyday Life,* Thomas Moore explains the importance of attention to the holy:

> Above all, a shrine gives presence to a felt but not always visible sentiment or realization. Significant intuitions and emotions about finding a place for the holy urge themselves toward some kind of expression, and a shrine comes into being. The shrine may be something quite ordinary, as when you visit a remarkable place, take some photographs, and then come home and hang a framed photograph of the place on the wall. That photograph is not only a reminder of a past experience; it also captures the spirit of the place and translates it to your home . . . Translation is a form of the word "transfer," and a shrine does indeed transfer the holiness of faith and whatever spirit is captured by sacred imagination to a particular place for memory and honor. (pp. 281–82)

Natural Fountains, Billy Goat Bluff, God's Mountain, Chapel Hill, and all the special locations that were secret and private to only a few became places of sacred, even holy, rituals. This was our growing up, our awakening, and our becoming. Many of us went on to find other holy places in the world, most notably in our homes and families: the raising and nurturing of children, the care of our communities, and the expression of ourselves as women, so necessary to the acceptance and celebration of the feminine.

That sacredness of place reinforced the sacredness of self. We did indeed lift our eyes unto the hills and not only found God, but a God who loved us enough to care for us, guide us, and nurture us throughout all the days of our going out and coming in again.

CHAPTER 10

I Corinthians 13

Though I speak with the tongues of men and of angels,
and have not charity, I am become as sounding brass,
or a tinkling cymbal.
And though I have the gift of prophesy, and understand all myster-
ies, and all knowledge; and though I have all faith,
so that I could move mountains, and have not charity,
I am nothing.
And though I bestow all my goods to feed the poor, and though I give
my body to be burned, and have not charity,
it profiteth me nothing.
Charity suffereth long, and is kind; charity envieth not;
charity vaunteth not itself, is not puffed up, doth not behave itself
unseemly, seeketh not her own, is not easily provoked, thinketh no
evil; rejoiceth not in iniquity, but rejoiceth in the truth; beareth all
things, believeth all things, hopeth all things, endureth all things.
Charity never faileth: but whether there be prophecies,
they shall fail; whether there be tongues, they shall cease; whether
there be knowledge, it shall pass away.
For we know in part, and we prophesy in part.
But when that which is perfect is come,
then that which is in part shall be done away.
When I was a child, I spake as a child,
I understood as a child, I thought as a child:
but when I became a man, I put away childish things.
For now we see through a glass, darkly; but then face to face: now I
know in part; but then shall I know
even as also I am known.
And now abideth faith, hope, charity, these three;
but the greatest of these is charity.

J attended a friend's wedding recently and, as at so many weddings, the thirteenth chapter of Saint Paul's letter to the Corinthians was read. This is a vision of perfect love, ideal love. However, most do not realize that this concept of charity is that of God's love, not human love. Unfortunately, humans do "seeketh their own," they can be "puffed up," they are likely to be provoked, and they have been known to envy others. Divine love, on the other hand, does not rejoice in evil; it bears all things, believes all things, and endures all things. Also, it is interesting that the King James Version of the Bible uses the word "charity" rather than "love," as is common in all other translations. Charity signifies a kind of love that is giving, one that regards the other as more important than the self. Perhaps that is more reminiscent of the type of love that God bestows on us.

When we in the modern age think of charity, we think of giving to the needy, of helping the poor or underpriviledged— but not anonymously. We will give, but at a price. We want to make sure it is tax deductible! God doesn't expect rewards, awards, or gold medals for his lovingkindness. All he asks of us is to love one another as ourselves, to love him alone as God, and to believe in the human-ness and divinity of his son, Jesus the Christ.

Not long ago I heard a story from a visiting pastor at our church. He told about a man who had died and was entering Heaven. He was in a long line with others, walking through the "pearly gates," greeted by Saint Peter. One by one, each person was introduced to God, the father, and Jesus, the Son of God. One man was overheard saying to the man in front of him, "So, that's what Jesus looks like!" The man at the end of the line walked up to Jesus, smiled, and said, "So. It was you all along."

As the scripture states, "we know in part . . . for now we see through a glass, darkly, but then face to face . . ." We know so little of God's plan and the mystery of life while we are living it. We see dimly, as through a dark mirror. But someday, in the presence of the Living God, we will comprehend the fullness of God's universe. The story by the visiting pastor illustrates that Christ is with us all the time. *We* are the body of Christ. *We* are members of the corporate body, and as we love one another, we love Him. When we come to true maturity, or in complete oneness with God in this life or in the next realm of life, we will see clearly. We will be known to ourselves, as we are known to God past, present, and future. God sees us as spiritual selves and, therefore, in perfection. We cannot achieve that perfection until, at last, we are united in presence and communion with him in the spiritual world.

There is a hymn by David Haas, which we sing at church:

We are the body of Christ,
broken and poured out,
promise of life from death,
we are the body of Christ.

We live so arrogantly. We think we are in control; we move mountains, re-channel rivers, cure diseases, and even create life in a test tube. We fool ourselves. We have the ability to fly faster than sound, yet we cannot defy the gravity that pulls us back to land. We have manufactured machines that can perform most any task, yet we have forgotten how to perform the most basic task . . . communicating with our loved ones. We cannot make it rain. We cannot command the clouds to go away when we have had too much rain. We are at the mercy of a force greater than we are; yet we dislike admitting that to ourselves, because we want to be in control. We have convinced ourselves that we are the new gods, that the machine is due all glory and honor. But none of this seems to matter when suddenly, without warning, we or someone we love is faced with tragedy, uncertainty, sadness, or calamity. Where do we turn when the unthinkable happens? When can we find comfort, solace, hope?

A number of years ago I was like Samuel in the Bible. I heard the call, but I did not recognize it.

And the child Samuel ministered unto the Lord before Eli. And the word of the Lord was precious in the days; there was no open vision. And it came to pass at that time, when Eli was laid down in his place, and his eyes began to wax dim, that he could not see. And ere the lamp of God went out in the temple of the Lord, where the ark of God was, and Samuel was laid down to sleep; That the Lord called Samuel; and he answered Here am I. And he ran unto Eli, and said, Here am I; for thou calledst me. And he said, I called not; lie down again. And he went and lay down. And the Lord called yet again, Samuel. And Samuel arose and went to Eli, and said, Here am I; for thou didst call me. And he answered, I called not, my son; lie down again. Now Samuel did not yet know the lord, neither was the word of the Lord yet revealed unto him. And the Lord called Samuel again the third time. And he arose and went to Eli, and said, Here am I; for thou didst call me. And Eli perceived that the Lord had called the child. Therefore Eli said unto Samuel, Go, lie down: and it shall be, if he call thee, that thou shalt say, Speak, Lord; for thy servant heareth. So Samuel went and lay down in his place. And the Lord came, and stood, and called as at other times, Samuel, Samuel. Then Samuel answered, Speak; for thy servant heareth. (KJV, 1 Sm. 3:1–10)

Sometimes the Lord calls us when we are most in need of his blessing, yet we may not recognize the voice. Simply put, the phone is ringing, but no one is at home.

Organized church had been, for me, a solitary experience. My parents saw to it that I went to Methodist youth group and attended church regularly, but I cannot recall a single time we went together. Yet I went, I sang, I prayed, and I believed.

After I married, our life seemed too busy for church, and so it was squeezed out for the sake of quality time together. Actually, we slept late on Sundays, the only day off from work, more often than we planned walks, picnics, or family time together. However, I thought I was happier than at any time in my adult life, and I couldn't have asked for anything more in my busy, well-planned, social life.

Then the unthinkable happened. After ten years of marriage, a marriage I thought was working quite well, my husband left me. I cried. I prayed. I bargained with God. I talked with a number of counselors; marriage counselors, psychological counselors, pastoral counselors, even sex counselors!

What happened? What had gone wrong? What was I going to do? Questions and more questions. I made up answers, wished for answers—feasible answers—and got no answers! I felt

113

like a deer caught in the headlights of an oncoming eighteen-wheeler. I didn't want to be alone again. I didn't want to be divorced. Not me!! I would not make the same mistakes my mother had made. I didn't want to die, but that was what it felt like, or maybe, for a time, that was what I wanted to happen to me.

I tried to return to church, but everything was too painful. My heart was broken, and my body ached, too. I felt as though all the skin had been stripped off my body, and even the air caused pain. When I taught my classes or met friends for dinner, I went through the motions. My life was on auto-pilot, except when I was at home and alone. There I found some peace in being where "we" had lived together. I deepened my pain, though, by resurrecting memories and trying to breathe life into them again.

One night I awakened from a disturbing dream. Sweat poured down my face, and I could hardly catch my breath. "I'm having a heart attack," I said out loud frantically. My entire body throbbed, and my heart boomed inside my chest. "Say the Lord's Prayer," I commanded. "Our Father, who art in heaven, hallowed..." I couldn't remember the next line. "Our Father," I began again, "who art in heaven, hallowed be thy name, and forgive us our sins as we forgive... No, that's not right," I cried. Trying to reassure myself that I was not having a heart attack was complicated by the fact that I couldn't recall the words of one of the most well-known prayers in Christendom.

Finally, I did remember the prayer, and I chanted it over and over again. I had not had a heart attack, merely a panic attack due to the stress of my situation. The next morning, a Sunday, I decided I had to do something to relieve my pain. I had listened to friends' advice, read countless "get back together"-type books, prayed for my husband to come home, and jogged myself senseless, and none of these offered a remedy to my suffering. I decided to try something else. Like Samuel, something called me, but I couldn't see the face or hear the voice clearly. I was looking through the dark glass for a vision of clarity. I had seen in part; now I needed to see distinctly.

I had been in Notre Dame Catholic Church only once before, when Frank Harrison, a devoted Catholic, died. I had never attended a Mass, but during a spiritual quest in my undergraduate years I privately visited a Catholic church, to pray and marvel at the beauty of that quiet, traditional house of worship.

That Sunday morning, I drove into town to church, not the church I was a member of, and not the church in which I had been married. That was still too painful. I didn't really know which church I was headed for. I just knew that I needed something and I thought I might find it in a church.

I was not fully conscious of the fact that I had turned right off Main Street, or that I had pulled into the Notre Dame parking lot. I got out of my car and walked toward the side entrance. All the faces were unfamiliar to me, but they looked friendly. A few people were talking beside the west entrance. I could hear laughter from around by the front door. Children ran and squealed on the lawn adjoining the parking lot. As I entered the church, there was an immediate contrast between the sultry temperature outside and the cool freshness inside. I caught a whiff of perfume, incense, and something that reminded me of newly mowed grass or morning honeysuckle. Greeters welcomed me as I stood in the foyer searching for a place where I could hide but still see the Mass. I was crying already, but no one noticed, or else they decided to leave me with my tears. No one was intrusive, yet I was received warmly.

I sat near the back row, and at the beginning of the Mass I heard the words, "Welcome to the celebration of the mystery of life." I thought to myself, "Celebration? I wish I had something to celebrate. Mystery? My marriage was a mystery." I was so focused on my own suffering and myself that I was missing the point of Faith, the reason for the Mass, and the purpose of fellowship. I had walked in on a celebration of all that was human including suffering, death, birth, eternal life, wonder, and the mystery of God. I was in the presence of the Divine, yet my attention to self was disconnecting me from the cure to my ailment.

John O'Donohue writes:

> It is often at the extremes that the eternal comes alive. When we are safely cushioned in our daily routine of duties and expectations, we forget who we are, and why it is that we are here. When suffering chooses you, the fabric of self-protection

tears. The old familiarities and securities fall away as if they had never been there. The raft of desires that guided daily life become utterly insignificant. Suddenly they seem like fantasies from another era. Every ounce of energy gathers into one intention: the desire to survive. In some subtle, animal sense, we always secretly know how precarious and vulnerable our presence here is. Suffering absolutely unveils this fragility. E. M. Cioran writes, "Without God, all is night, with him light is useless." (p. 189)

As I began to listen to the readings and the homily, and to repeat the familiar words of the Nicene Creed and the Lord's Prayer, I was surprised at how personal it sounded. I was not hearing these words for the first time, yet I felt as though I was a stranger welcomed into an unknown land. The words and the Word spoke to me. I sensed that my name was called. I stopped crying and I listened, marveling at the intimacy of the message.

For weeks thereafter, I continued to attend Mass at Notre Dame, always alone and always sitting in the back near an easy retreat. I was still embarrassed by my near-constant flow of tears, but no one else seemed to notice. Later Father Mike assured me, "If you can't cry openly in church, where can you?"

One Sunday I noticed in the weekly bulletin an announcement that read, "For anyone interested in deepening their faith, finding out more about the Catholic faith, or becoming Catholic please contact..." RCIA stood for the Rite of Christian Initiation for Adults.

For most of my life, church had been a solitary activity. I went by myself, prayed by myself, left by myself, and went home by myself. Throughout my marriage, that had not changed. So, I decided to attend the classes, which met every Tuesday night for nine months. At first I had no plans to change my denomination. I was curious about Catholicism and had been for much of my adult life. But as I became a part of a community in which others were seeking direction on their own personal faith journeys, attitudes began to change. I began to change.

The summer I was separated, I decided I needed a change of scenery for a few weeks. I flew out to California to visit an old friend from graduate school. The California landscape did me good. There were no reminders of my life in Texas, no lingering memories of the chasm that had divided my home and my dreams of a lifelong union. We shopped, saw movies, giggled, and chatted like the old friends we were, and then, sometimes late into the evening, my friend consoled me when a flood of tears broke through without warning.

I dreaded going home. I knew I had to face the reality of divorce; separate property, separate lives, severed dreams. I chose a window seat on the plane and settled into what I hoped would be a flight with no turbulence (I've always hated to fly!), and one without any conversation with strangers.

Just before the plane doors were closed and secured, a man, a latecomer, came tramping down the aisle. "Oh, please don't sit next to me," I pleaded silently. Of course, he did sit next to me and starting talking immediately. I tried to be polite but indicated that I was not interested in conversation. He persisted. "What's you name? Where are your from? Where are you going? Did you like California?"—a litany of perfunctory questions.

I answered, "Claudia. Texas. Texas. Yes," offering no more information than I had to in order to bring closure to this exchange.

He droned on, telling me about his wife and three children, who were seated somewhere in the back of the plane, about his work, and how much he had traveled. He even tried to get me involved in a discussion of the California penal system, but I offered no comment. Then came the question, "So, tell me, Claudia. Are you married?" He must have seen the tears welling up in my eyes. I quickly diverted my attention to the snowy clouds outside the window. He got the message. He whispered, "I'm sorry," and patted my arm. "Divorced?" he said with sincere sensitivity.

"Almost," I uttered in a quivering voice. Finally, he was silent. I slept until the steward arrived with lunch.

At first we ate our lunch without exchange. The silence must have been awkward for both of us, because we started to speak at the same time. Laughter broke the tension and we began to talk, this time with me as an equal partner. I told him about my work as a college teacher, and my love for animals, dogs and horses, especially. I brought up the subject of religion and explained that I was in the RCIA program at my church. He laughed broadly and said, "Oh I'm a *roving* Catholic, not a Roman Catholic."

"I guess we're all on a search," I said and smiled at him.

For a few moments we entered into a serious religious discussion. Who was God? How did He intervene in our lives? Did He hear and answer prayer? How could He let bad things like divorce, happen? The man seemed like a person of faith, great energy, and uncontrolled optimism. He suddenly had a thought, and as he spoke he faced me, took both my hands in his, and said plainly and intently, "Claudia, the Lord's plan is unfolding before you!" We were locked in one another's gaze. I didn't know what to say. I wanted to believe him, but who *was* this man, after all? As quickly as he let go of my hands, the announcement came over the P.A. to prepare for landing. We exchanged no other words except to say good-bye, good luck, and nice meeting you.

The flight was over, and I was on my way home again, but because he seemed to believe what he said to me, I began to believe it, too. Maybe God's plan was unfolding before me at that very moment, in every moment of my life.

So many people assisted me on my journey back from grief and loss. One time Father Mike asked me, "How do you think God feels when love fails?" I knew how I felt, and somehow I was comforted by the thought that God, Jesus, all the saints, everyone had suffered some kind of unfathomable loss, had found hope again, and ultimately found new meaning in life and love. I knew that I could do that, too.

The culmination of the RCIA journey comes during the season of Lent. Lent is, for Christians, a time of contemplation, meditation, and of reconciliation. For Catholics it is a time to bring converts into the full fold of the church. On the night before Easter Sunday, the Easter fires are lit, the ancient words are proclaimed, and all the steps of preparation have been completed, and in a glorious celebration there is baptism, confirmation, and Eucharist (communion).

That night my Lenten season came to an end. Symbolic-

118

ally, I had been living my own Lenten season; a time of casting away, a time of drought, a time of preparation for the coming life. With the help, support, and love of a caring community, I was able to celebrate the spring. I realized that we need to experience a lenten season, a season when we embark on a new journey, take a few steps, stop, look around, wonder, question, take a step back, then forward again, but always toward some goal of authenticity, self-awareness, and wholeness.

My life was saved. Now I wake to "Good Morning, Lord!" instead of "Good Lord, it's morning!" I saw the dark glass and put it away as with other things of childhood so that I could see clearly and as an adult. The seeds of faith, which had been planted so many years before at camp, now had come to full fruition. Faith and hope are important, but nothing exists without the love that binds all things together.

The love that exists between the divine and human can only be realized when we, the human, seek out the divine. God is omnipresent, that is, always waiting for us to knock at the door, extend a needy hand, or call his name. We are called to live our lives as a sacrament, acknowledging our existence as both a profound mystery and a sacred presence.

Djohariah Toor proclaims:

> The more we experience this transformation, the more authentic our lives become. It doesn't matter how incomplete our past has been, what abuse or neglect we have experienced, or how powerful our shadow or unconscious our behaviors. When we fully accept and embrace our broken-ness, then we can turn to work on our wholeness. In spite of our personal or relational tragedy, we can choose to say to God, "Teach me to dance!" Our awakening lies in the choice. (p. 208)

More than thirty years ago, I gave a talk (based on words by Dr. Sam Junkin, President of Schreiner College) at camp during the counselor vespers service. It is one of the most anticipated and lovely services during the camp term. All the counselors, dressed in white, line up near the waterfront, each one holding a lighted candle set in a wooden base. Certain counselors speak on subjects drawn from the letters in the

119

word M Y S T I C. That year my letter was "C," and I chose to speak on courage. As nightfall crept across the river, each counselor gently set her candle on a watery pilgrimage following the dying sun reflected in the glassy surface. Prayers, secret wishes, promises, and private invocations go along with each sailing candle.

I have saved those words spoken so long ago. The paper is yellowed, curled, and frayed around the edges, yet its message still speaks of "lenten" reflection:

We have mountains of ignorance and immaturity to be moved . . . and we have moved many mountains.

We have bridges of wisdom and integrity to be built . . . and we have built them.

We have distant horizons of knowledge and human understanding to be explored . . . and we have explored them.

And none of these are easy tasks, so take courage.

No human endeavor will stand the final test of authenticity if insulated from personal risk, so take courage.

Giving, helping, serving . . .

All of these are full of risks.

We risk ourselves, our own fragile self-concepts when we try to help some one grow . . .

Maybe they won't understand our care.

Maybe they won't accept our attempts to try.

Maybe they will reject what we have carefully given.

Maybe no one will ever understand what we crammed of ourselves in those steps we took to serve.

I cannot thank you by giving you courage, but courage is yours to take.

Take it as a free gift from God.

And if the meaning of our corporate and individual lives has already been discovered, we may color our existence with the somber tones of despair.

There is an exciting future, a future worth anticipating, a future which is more stimulating than either past or present.

So take hope my friend! Take hope!

Jesus Christ, Lord of the past and present, works before us making all things new.

We need not be afraid when we face new questions, or

imposing threats, or even when we seem to persist in dreaming the impossible dreams.

We dare to believe at Mystic that we work in concert with him following as he leads, so take hope.

Take the challenge with courage and hope.

Take the challenge even if it means going down difficult and lonely roads.

Take the challenge and know that God has a beautiful plan for each of us.

CHAPTER 11

The Prayer of a Sportsman

Dear Lord, in the battle that goes on through life,
I ask but a field that is fair.
A chance that is equal with all in the strife,
a courage to strive and to dare.
And if I should win, let it be by the code,
with my faith and my honor held high.
And if I should lose, let me stand by the road,
and cheer as the winners go by.
And Lord, may my shouts be ungrudging and clear,
a tribute that comes from the heart.
And let me not cherish a snarl or a sneer,
or play any sniveling part.
Let me say, "There they ride on laurels bestowed,
since they played the game better than I."
Let me stand with a smile by the side of the road,
and cheer as the winners go by.
So, grant me to conquer, if conquer I can,
by proving my worth in the fray,
but teach me to lose like a regular man,
and not like a craven, I pray.
Let me take my hat off to the warriors who strode
to victory splendid and high.
Yet teach me to stand by the side of the road,
and cheer as the winners go by.

The modern Olympics are symbolized by joined, colored rings. At camp, our competitive spirit is symbolized by the colors of the two tribes, the Tonkawas and the Kiowas. On the first night of a camper's first year, she, along with a hundred other new campers, draws a colored slip of paper out of a hat. If she draws a blue slip, she is "ever-loyal" Kiowa for the remainder of her camping days. When a red slip is drawn, she is "true" Tonk.

Throughout the camp term, the Tonks and Kiowas meet every Tuesday, Thursday, and Saturday afternoon to engage in friendly but fierce competition in a variety of sports from junior dodgeball and intermediate softball to senior volleyball and track and field. Campers not selected for the teams for their age group stand by and cheer, usually holding branches stripped from the nearest tree, used as pom-pons. They yell and yelp, "Smash 'em, kick 'em, and bury 'em." Discarded tennis-ball cans filled with gravel make for annoying shakers, and painted signs forebode the demise of the losing team. Tribe games are serious stuff! But when the game is over and winning teams are surrounded with cheers of congratulations and losing teams are assured there is a "next time," campers come together again as friends, as cabinmates, and walk arm in arm toward Chapel Hill for a time of quiet. The competitive boundaries are quickly forgotten, and the prospect of being a winner or loser seems less important than being a good friend.

The Olympics attempt to do this in the world at large. They try to say, "We live in one world with one another. Shouldn't we try to be friends and understand one another, just a little bit? Shouldn't we try to let our spirit of nationalism spill out onto the soccer field, or hockey field, instead of the battlefield? We are, after all, humans first, and members of individual countries second."

We learned this lesson easily at camp. One camper recalls:

I remember The Prayer of a Sportsman. I remember all too well the huge lump in my throat when the Kiowas lost a big game to the Tonks. Iney would read the prayer a few times each term. The Tonks would shake hands with us and say,

123

"Good game," and the Kiowas would rally round their teammates. We knew we had lost but we were still proud. We would say to one another, "You played great," but sometimes inside you knew you could have played better, worked harder, but after awhile it didn't seem to matter anyway. When the Kiowas won a big game against the Tonks we would go over to them and say "Good game," and try to ease the lumps in their throats. I remember going to Chapel Hill after tribe games. I always felt like God was probably sitting there next to me and making me feel whole, or proud, or maybe at peace with myself. By the time dinner came around no one was talking about the game. We were talking about what was coming up next. I guess we learned the meaning of "friendly competition" from the prayer and from our own experience. (Sullivan, pp. 45-46)

The spirit of sportsmanship is not stressed enough in today's competitive activities.We don't see evidence of good sportsmanship often enough in today's professional sports, or even in little league sports involving boy and girls as young as five. We have all heard stories of overzealous parents being ejected from games because they harassed the umpire or another parent. Perhaps we were lucky that parents seldom witnessed our tribal games at camp. Unfortunately, there are a few cases of parent-against-parent violence over a score in a game. Can you imagine a parent taking physical action against another parent, or umpire, or coach because their child was taken out of a game or missed a point? At Mystic we had much to lose by defeat, yet we knew we had much more to gain in accepting that defeat graciously.

Honor. Faith. Personal courage. Testing the limits. Perseverance. The seeds of these values were planted in each camper, and, as the parable suggests, the receptivity of the seed determined the outcome of it fruition:

Behold, a sower went forth to sow; and when he sowed, some seeds fell by the way side, and the fowls came and devoured them up: some fell upon stony places, where they had not much earth: and forthwith they sprung up, because they had no deepness of earth: and when the sun was up, they were scorched; and because they had no root, they

124

withered away. And some fell among thorns; and the thorns sprung up, and choked them; but others fell into good ground, and brought forth fruit, some a hundredfold, some sixtyfold, some thirtyfold. (Mt. 13:3-8)

Whenever a camper couldn't let go of the loss of a game, it was usually because she doubted or blamed herself. Bearing the entire burden of loss on one's shoulders can be a terrific load. Oftentimes the weight of winning or losing was placed on the more athletic girls. Many campers played sports in their schools or for city league teams. At camp they were known for their athletic prowess and admired for their skills. The remainder of us, who excelled in ballet, gymnastics, horseback riding, makeup, and boys were relegated to the sidelines, where we cheered, offered moral support, and served as "water girls" for the members of the team. I, fortunately or not, was one of those campers who seldom was selected for a team. Not that I was uncoordinated or unathletic, quite the contrary, but I was far more interested in drama, dance, horseback riding, and swimming than in what we called "landsports." However, I do recall times that a few "weenies" (a term used to describe someone who was non-athletic) were chosen for certain teams. Each tribe elected "sportsmanagers" to pick team members, instruct them in the rules of the particular sport, and to coach them into a winning team. Either some sportsmanagers recalled what it was like to be overlooked, or else they succumbed to a gentle heart and gave some camper the chance of her life . . . to be on a team.

When you are eight or twelve, shy and a bit withdrawn, unsure of your place in the world, much less that of a summer-camp "Junior Steal the Bacon" team, game day might as well be the Super Bowl. You wake up antsy and excited. You pick at your breakfast and go through the motions during morning classes. Rest hour comes, and it is endless! You can't wait until that afternoon and the game. Finally, the time comes. You are decked out in your blue and white, or red and white. You have secret letters painted on your forearm or on a strand of ribbon tied around your forehead. 'TWWWTS' (Tonks Will Win With Tonk Spirit) or 'KFND' (Kiowa Fight Never Die)

Before the game you gather with your teammates for

125

prayer, then it's off to the field. You are as pumped up as you have ever been in your life. It's your time to shine. All the camp is amassed to watch you and your fellow "Steal the Bacon-ers" challenge one another on the field of competition.

You line up in selected order and wait to hear your number called. Your body is tense, every muscle primed for the moment when you break away, run into the center, steal the bacon (an eraser or rubber "O"), and sprint back across your home line to score a point.

Suddenly, you hear your number! You dash. Your entire focus is on the bacon (eraser). You reach for it the exact second your opponent touches it, grabs it, and runs toward her line. You strive with every ounce of strength to tag her, but, alas, she is faster than you are, or perhaps she got a split-second headstart on you. You are shattered. The other side got the point. Now you must walk back to your line . . . shaken . . . disappointed . . . and humiliated. Teammates greet you. "Good job," from one, a pat on the back and, "Next time," from another. "Almost," assures one. "Smile," commands the sports-manager. You feel spent, but elevated, because you went beyond what you thought you could accomplish. "Next time," you say to yourself, gritting your teeth.

How many young campers had a similar experience? How many young women learned for the first time that they could push themselves past what they thought, or had been convinced, were their limits?

The greatest competitive challenge at camp came with the War Canoe race presented at closing activities each term. Senior campers who excelled in watersports tried out for the war-canoe class, and thus began work toward the final race some five weeks away. Girls thirteen through seventeen years of age labored through extensive and exhausting land drills: sprints, stretches, squat thrusts, precision drills, and water drills: deep-water strokes, quick starts, and backwater drills.

As the camp term drew near an end, each war canoe, which held ten oarsmen and one stern, received a fresh coat of red or blue paint. Each member of the boat painstakingly lettered her initials on the outside of the boat near her position. The crews of each boat selected symbolic names for their crafts . . . *Mariah,* for the wind, . . . *Thunderbolt,* for the strength of nature, . . . or *Shalom,* for peace. Campers worked for weeks on a precision ceremonial salute, to be performed at the beginning of the race. The boats were treated with great respect, almost with reverence, each time they were lifted from the water by members of the crew. They held the heavy aluminum boats high above their heads and pounded out a rhythmic beat on the side of the boat, all the while bellowing and chanting in ritualistic fervor.

Race day arrives, marking the beginning of closing activities and the appearance of Mom and Dad (and little brother, cocker spaniel, and artifacts from civilization). Campers, who just days before had pledged their undying love and loyalty to Mystic, quickly forget their oaths, finding another loyalty instead in the awaiting arms of Mommy and Daddy. The war-canoe crews, on the other hand, have only one thing on their minds . . . *the race.* In many cases they instruct their parents not to find them until after the race. They have worked too long and too hard to be diverted from their prime goal . . . *winning.*

Parents, other visitors, campers, counselors, and staff assemble under the pecan trees near the waterfront. It is evident that anyone from the "outside world" is alien to this environment. There are secret chants and special handshakes, and every camper wears some significant gear—painted head ribbons, a T-shirt with a boat's name, and tribe colors. As the swimming and diving competitions are completed, the war canoes are lowered lovingly into the water. Campers take their positions, five on port, five on starboard, and one stern. The girls wear looks too serious for their ages. The stern exhibits her painted oar, a kind of talisman that, hopefully, will ensure victory.

Each boat oars past the crowd, then aims in straight to the docks, holding water (a kind of treading of water where oars are in the water but the boat does not move). The stern beats out a strong rhythm by pounding her oar onto the bottom of the boat. The ceremonial salute begins. Oars wave out in a fan pattern with exact precision, then each one is carefully handed over from bow-mate to bow-mate. The salute ends with all oars crashing down on the sides of the boat, giving it an appearance of some strange prehistoric insect primed for flight. The stern shouts in a commanding voice, "Hold water!" There is a deafening pause. "Starboard . . . back water. Port . . . ceremonial stroke. And . . . sttroooke!" The repeated cry of "Stroke!" can be heard until the boat is far downriver near the starting line, and the next boat sweeps in for its salute.

The moment arrives, and both boats are lined up at the large silver-colored buoys near the dam. Waterfront counselors hold the crafts steady, making sure they are evenly lined. No longer are these the tender, pubescent campers from Shady Shack, Seventh Heaven, and Idiot's Delight. They are women ready for the race of their lives. Look closely and you can see jaws clenched in determination, shoulder and back muscles tense and taut, eyes riveted ahead, toward the finish line downriver. There is a steady scream from the shore, "Counselors away!" Counselors holding the boats dive and swim immediately for the murky bottom of the Guadalupe, out of the ferocious force of eleven paddles propelling each boat in the first, deep, labored, reaching stroke. The race has begun.

Defeats can be bitter experiences, especially when you feel you have much to lose and many to disappoint. At all the finish lines, and all of the last innings, and all the set points there are winners and losers. There are tears of joy and crushing tears of defeat. Yet we go on. We prepare for the next game, or the next tournament, or maybe we realize that this was our last game. We will never enter the field in quite the same way again. That is part of growing up . . . learning to let go.

One of the important lessons we learned at camp was that there comes a time to let go of some of the dreams of childhood. Childish things let go of themselves, but the dreams of childhood, which can at times be dreams of grandiosity, must fall away like last season's leaves, which must, in time, be replaced with a new season's lavish splendor.

My childhood dreams were that I would never have to leave camp. I wished for it always to be summer. Never-Never Land should have been real. I believed it was, while I was sheltered there alongside that sparkling water, nestled within rocky canyons, at play in open meadows, and at home with all that surrounded me. I reluctantly let go of my Never-Never Land, but instead I kept the dream of water, the rugged hills, and nature close by. Whether it was fate or the intentions of my unconscious, I made my home, ultimately, a few miles from Mystic's front gate.

My first home after I married was just across the highway from the river and only four miles from the place of my summer memories and my childhood dreams. On clear, windless, summer nights I could almost hear the whirring fans and the trailing sounds of those sweet voices calling "Goodnight" from one cabin to the next.

We left the best parts of our youth there at camp. We gave, and learned, and grew, and transformed ourselves into something none of us could have planned, yet nothing that any of us would have been surprised at becoming. As each of us traveled back into the world, we took priceless gifts with us: gifts as varied and precious as the gifts presented to the young Christ child. The gifts bestowed upon him were for the journey: the journey that became his life, a life that changed the world. One person, just one, changed the world—and all because there were people who believed in him, his message, and the goodness that he sought for all human beings. His gifts were gold, the most precious; frankincense, the rarest; and myrrh, the most bitter.

Our gifts were less prophetic, yet they prepared us for the way. Many of us became doctors, lawyers, pastors, and teachers. Most became wives and mothers. All became women who, because of the camp experience, were better prepared to handle whatever task, responsibility, duty, or charge was placed in their lives.

From living together we learned patience, forgiveness, compassion, and respect for one another. Sometimes working together does produce better and faster results. I am reminded of the "work chart" that was placed in each cabin, made from two cardboard pie plates. On the outside of one plate was written a series of duties: sweep aisle, mop aisle, sweep bathroom, mop bathroom, empty trash, and so on. On the inside circle from the other plate were written the names of each camper. A shiny brass brad held the plates together so that the names or the duties could be shifted once a day. Today I mop. Tomorrow Susie sweeps, and so on until all the chores are completed and every camper has a specified duty. Sometimes a camper received a phone message, or had to go by the infirmary to take a morning medication, or lingered after breakfast and therefore missed her chore. Some other camper always stepped in and did two chores that day, just so the entire cabin wouldn't lose points on the inspections check. That was quite a lesson for an eight-year-old who may have never been instructed in using the working end of a broom or mop!

From the tribe activities we learned courage, perseverance, the importance of teamwork, sportsmanship, and leadership. Each camper had a way of contributing to her tribe's points, which were tallied at the end of camp to determine the "winner of the term." Maybe you never made a team. Maybe you never ran a race or swam a lap. You could, however, win points in Arts and Crafts class by designing the best enameled jewelry, or by winning a ribbon in the Horse Show, or even by singing in the tribe choir or dancing in tribe dance. Everyone had a place and a possibility of giving to the whole, no matter their age or the popularity of the competition.

Campers and counselors acquired much from living in contact with one another. Counselors learned basic parenting and teaching skills by living with campers in cabins and by teaching classes. How important it was to be admired, respected, and looked up to at the age of eighteen or nineteen! I remember what it meant to me the first time I heard a young camper say to me, "When I grow up I want to be just like you." The late teen years can be a formidable time when one's sense of self is being developed and tested, not to mention that many teens haven't learned to be at ease with themselves by that age. By living in a close environment with young girls, counselors are invited to re-experience their own innocence, rediscover their lost sense of naivete and childlike simplicity.

For campers who did not have sisters or appropriate role models, the counselor could be a powerful, and, at times, daunting figure. One night my first year as counselor to twenty seven-year-olds, I heard terrifying screams coming from the bathroom. Girls of that age seem to do everything together and as was the case, they were all in the shower, near the shower, or just exiting the shower. I ran into the bathroom ready to save the day, since that was how I perceived my job at that time, and found twenty wet, naked, screaming, wriggling little girls. At first I couldn't make out just exactly what the problem was. They were making such a racket, and none of them seemed to be going anywhere. They just slid and squealed and jumped up and down. Finally, I discerned the word, "Scorpion!" I was terrified of the grisly little creatures myself. How could I save these innocent children from the minute monster that had struck such fear in their hearts and lungs? "Okay!" I shouted. "Everybody out of the shower." They "eeuu-ed" and "guuee-ed" and "eeegh-ed" until they were all in a huddle at the opposite end of the bathroom near the closet. Their shivering, panting little bodies created such commotion that, by now, there were two counselors from adjoining cabins come to see what the excitement was all about.

I slowly stepped into the communal shower, flashlight and broom in hand, searching for the legged demon, and there, crawling up the side of the shower wall was not one, but five or six of the little devils. Quickly, with one deft swoop of the broom, they were sent to a watery grave and down the drain. "Ah, the world is safe again, at last," I thought to myself. Now I just had to convince the campers that all was well and that they could resume their showers.

Later, all clean and dressed for bed, each camper added her prayer to the petitions of that evening. "Thank you, God, for Camp Mystic and all my friends," one said quietly. "And bless my parents and my brother, and my dog," added another. "And please God, don't send any more scorpions to our cabin." We all sighed, "Amen."

131

CHAPTER 12

The Serenity Prayer

God, grant me the courage to change the things I can;
The serenity to accept the things I cannot change,
And the wisdom to know the one from the other.

Unlike other prayers spoken or sung at camp, the Serenity Prayer was seldom heard. In fact, I don't recall ever hearing it; rather it was written in blank books decorated for some special friend, or postscripted at the end of a letter or note. The Serenity Prayer did not come from the sacred liturgies of our churches, or from the Young Life movement that had so captured many of the teens of those days. This prayer was truly secular, growing from a movement few of us had heard of or experienced firsthand by those tender years.

I grew up as a child of an alcoholic parent, and I had heard of AA (Alcoholics Anonymous), but I never associated any of that dysfunction with my time at camp. Yet, from time to time, a line or two from that prayer would find its way into some "pep talk" or conversation pertaining to a particular personal challenge.

How can I change what needs to be changed? How can I come to terms with those things I cannot change? And how can I know the difference between what can and should be changed and those that are better left alone?

Persistent questions. Difficult answers.

Sometimes the first thing to be changed is me: my attitude, my outlook, my perception of self as it relates to others. This can be the most challenging personal task some may ever

132

face. My second year as a counselor, I lived in Hangout with intermediate campers ages eleven and twelve. We had a tight-knit group, many of whom had been together since their first year at camp four years before. The closeness of our cabin was soon to be challenged, however, by a camper named Carole, who was moved from another cabin to ours because she wasn't getting along with her group.

Carole was an extraordinarily beautiful child with flaming red hair that flowed in long tresses past her hips. Her face was delicate: a fragile mouth, pert nose, and clear, piercing green eyes. Freckles lightly dusted her face and shoulders. Her body was lean and girlish, and she moved with impish energy. Whenever I saw her running, she reminded me of Tinkerbell, and because of that fairy-like quality, I realized that she was the first "true spirit" I had ever known.

She was honest in displaying her emotions, yet with words she could be deceitful and manipulative. Apparently she came from a wealthy family who traveled a great deal. Her father was an executive for DuPont. "Dad is in South America, my brother is in our apartment in New York, and I don't know where my mom is right now," she explained with an air of no concern. They had lived in South America, Greece, and New York. She seemed alone in the world, independent, yet she was searching for something, too. Her independent spirit and ingeniously creative nature set her apart from the rest of the twelve-year-olds. Her world travels and exposure to sophisticated adults (and adult situations) sent a message of snobbery to the other campers, and they reacted with shock and aloofness, as though she was some sort of threat to their own desire for acceptance. She was a castaway, and although she hated not being accepted by the group, her way of dealing with it was simply to say, verbally and non-verbally, "I don't give a darn if you like me or not." And so the others preferred not to like her.

Carole came to our cabin because she was in the production of *Peter Pan* I was directing that term and we had become friends. We did share, after all, a similar interest in theatre, acting, and dance. She was cast in the part of Tiger Lily, and she was as natural a young actress as I had ever seen. Onstage

133

she could be bold, focused, intelligent, and precise beyond her years or experience. Dance... she never missed a step. Sing... she never missed a note. Act... her Tiger Lily was spunky, cute, assertive, and wholly charming. In most cases in which a camper excelled, others would applaud and be supportive. In Carole's case, the other campers became jealous, envious, and quarrelsome.

At times Carole's innocence came as a surprise to me. She had probably seen, done, and experienced more in her twelve years than I had at nineteen. It was clear from her conversation that she had an awkward knowledge of sex, reproduction, drugs, and boys, and she was not in the least bit shy in sharing what she knew, or thought she knew.

Those were days before the so-called "Youth Movement" exploded with its new love, psychedelic drugs, student power, and warning of "Don't trust anyone over thirty." At least we in the Midwest and South were spared the early start of the revolution. Nonetheless, we were aware of the stereotyping and the new lingo. Carole was quickly labeled "hippie," a title she wore with obvious pleasure. Amongst counselors she was called "brat," "uncontrollable," and "rotten." She was the first to wear tie-dyed T-shirts, cutoff jeans, a Haight-Ashbury hat, and love beads. She often refused to do her cabin chores, claiming, "I don't need to know how to do that sort of thing. I'll have the maid do it." The campers did not take kindly to being likened to "maids."

Further evidence of her precociousness was her ability to slip away, almost unnoticed, and wander off into the hills. This, of course, sent harried counselors running to Iney, crying, "I've lost one of my campers!" Carole wasn't lost. She simply couldn't be found—that is, until she wanted to be, or until she tired of the wanderlust and came back of her own will.

I suppose I saw a side of myself in Carole. As she ran across the Flats on her way to a waterfront class with the wind in her vibrant red hair, she looked like some great untamed filly at once in love with her wildness and longing to be tamed by something, by someone. There was in her a yearning to belong, a deep desire to be a part of something permanent and

134

secure. That was the point of identification I secretly shared with her.

At the counselors' bidding, the campers of Hangout did try to include Carole, at least at first. During nighttime devotionals, the topic of "friendship" was used to promote a more positive attitude toward our newcomer. The campers were reaching out, but it was Carole who remained tentative and somehow withdrawn. Had she been hurt before? Did she know the pain of rejection at such an early age? Why was she so reluctant to take the hands she so desperately wanted to hold?

Against my better judgment, I sometimes allowed Carole to come out onto the cabin landing after Taps to sit and talk awhile. All the other campers were asleep, or supposed to be, and this was a special time for counselors to relax, sneak a cigarette or candy bar, and just be alone. I decided Carole could use the extra attention, so I invited her outside and we talked about the play, about her travels, and about her life. I admit that I was fascinated, in the beginning, by the stories of her adventures in Greece, South America, and in private school in New York. I tried to broach the subject of "getting along" with the others, but her excitement only grew as she crafted tales of a near kidnapping, sexual encounters with boys, and one particular fantasy she called "the red devil." I was never quite sure if these stories were products of an overactive imagination, paranoia, drug-induced fantasy, or simply dreams.

The story of the red devil came up over and over again, and she told it with such conviction that it was clear she believed her own concoction. The red devil, it seemed, would visit her at night, threatening to take her away to some hell-like den. He was ferocious, with overt sexual overtones. As she told the story, her intensity increased to an almost hysterical pitch. More than once I grabbed her by the shoulders, shook her, and said in no uncertain terms, "Stop it now. I don't believe a word you are saying." Exhausted with her fantasy and tired of the manipulative game, she quieted. We talked awhile longer about what we wanted to be when we grew up, about the persistent parental angst, and about camp. She loved the place, as I did, but she connected with the natural world instead of the human one, and that left her wanting.

For my birthday that August she got special permission (again) from Iney to take me to a place "off limits" to the rest of camp. It was the area below the dam, which was not part of Mystic's property. She cajoled Iney into letting us venture to that place of roaring waters, maidenhair fern, and a riverbed that had carved out channels just large enough for one to fit snuggly into, hence the name "the bath tubs."

During rest hour, when everyone else was napping, writing their boyfriends, or reading the latest Archie comics, Carole and I hiked to the tubs for my private birthday celebration. I never figured out how Carole did it, but she had somehow procured a Mexican delicacy called *sucre dulce*. It resembled a sugarcoated sugar cane, sweet and grainy, chewy and delicious. We washed our hair in the river, feeling like we were in some Hawaiian paradise rather than in the Texas Hill Country. We laughed and giggled as small fish nipped at the unshaved hair on our legs. This special time together was, in part, her birthday gift. Just before it was time to return to camp, she presented me with something that she had found in one of those books of poetry shared among friends at camp. She had written it out on a piece of handmade paper, and she began to read aloud:

> We have met strangers among strangers searching for meaning through people and experiences.
> Loneliness had been our companion like a suitcase of past adventures carried with us providing some security.
> Our adventure provided warmth, an added dimension to our lives. We gave to each other even though it wasn't expected. Between passing days and fleeting romances our friendship has grown, never defined by words.
> Because of the way you are I have wanted to give you a gift.
> Flowers would have added warmth for moments, but nothing tangible can last forever.
> Nothing I have to give would represent my true feelings for you.
> Finally, one day clustered among the colorful aspens

and the sounds of a rushing brook, I discovered my gift for you.

All that I can give you is time . . . time to grow . . . to share . . . to love . . . as only you can.

My demands of you are simple. Blossom, my friend, into the beautiful flower I see inside. Share your warmth, as you love. Spread your happiness as you give, and remember me as I pass through your mind like gentle waves on the drifting sand.

Love, Carole

"How could this child have such depth?" I wondered. Did I tame her wildness, or had she imparted some of it to me? The beauty of the words warmed me throughout, sending a wave of chills over my sun-drenched body. I had no words adequate to respond. I only smiled with tears edging near the corners of my eyes. "You go on ahead," I suggested to her, embarrassed by my emotions. "I'll catch up with you in a few minutes. I want to be alone here for a bit," I said. She turned to go without a murmur, stepping up the rocky slope that led to the top of the dam. For a moment I studied the water cascading over the dam, looking like liquid glass. The foamy spray sprinkled my face with tiny droplets that cooled and soothed my sunburned face and arms. There was not enough time to fully take in the loveliness of the afternoon, and there was no time to linger any longer. I set out toward the top of the dam and the green expanse that led back to Hangout.

Just as I reached the dam and was once again on level ground I bent down to re-tie my shoe. I heard, as though from a far distance, a voice calling my name. "Claudia," it called softly, almost inaudibly. I looked up and, at first, could see no one. Again I heard my name, this time a little closer. Now I could see her. It was Carole, and she was running toward me, arms outstretched. She moved as though in extreme slow motion, seconds between the landing of one foot then the other. I heard the high-pitched song of a killdeer as it skimmed the river's surface. At the same instant, wind moved across my face like a giant hand, tousling my hair so that I couldn't see. By the time I seized the swirling locks, shaking them from my eyes, I caught sight of her again, this time almost as she reached me. She half jumped into my embrace, and we both laughed as we struggled to maintain balance. "I'm glad you're my friend," she blurted out. "And I'm glad I'm at camp. Happy birthday." Again I was speechless. I was trying to make sense of the last few moments: the seeming time lapse, the illusion of slow motion, the transformation I had witnessed in her, and, more importantly, the one I felt happening inside of me. Later, when I recalled the story to an older counselor, she replied simply, "That's what they call mysticism. You've experienced mysticism."

Mysticism. There was that word again. I had heard it often whenever a camper or counselor chose to interpret the letter "M" in some talk at devotionals or vespers. Mysticism is an ancient term used to describe a spirit of oneness with nature, God, others, or the universe. Madeleine L'Engle, in *Walking on Water,* suggests:

> Long before Jung came up with his theories of archetypal understanding, William James wrote: "Our lives are like islands in the sea, or like trees in the forest, which comingle their roots in the darkness underground. Just so, there is a continuum of cosmic consciousness, against which our individuality builds but accidental fences, and into which our several minds plunge as into a mother sea or reservoir."
>
> The creator is not afraid to leap over the "accidental fences," and to plunge into the deep waters of creation. There, once again, and in yet another way, we lose ourselves to find ourselves. (p. 90)

The fact is, we are all connected to all that is, or ever was, or will ever be. The earth beneath our feet, the birds of the air, the teeming waters of the ocean fed by the rivers and streams that run near our houses are all a part of creation, just as we are a component of that creation. I cannot be separated from all that lives or has ever lived. God has promised us that in what we now know as genetic science. Even the Bible lists the human ancestors of Jesus, proving a living chain from the beginning of time until today and on to forever.

Again L'Engle prompts us:

138

Sitting, or, better, lying on one of my favorite sun-warmed rocks, I try to take time to let go, to listen in much the same way that I listen when I am writing. This is praying time, and the act of listening in prayer is the same act as listening in writing. And again, comparisons need not come into it; the prayer of the saint is not necessarily "better" than the prayer of the peasant.

And then there is time in which to be, simply to be, that time in which God quietly tells us who we are and who he wants us to be. It is then that God can take our emptiness and fill it up with what he wants, and drain away the business with which we inevitably get involved in the dailiness of human living. (p. 170)

I was often reminded at camp that we are human *beings* and not human *doings*. It can be difficult simply to be. We are so patterned to accomplishment, attaining goals, and checking off things from our "To Do" lists. True prayer is not petitioning God or even praising God. It is *being* with God as two old friends sitting by the water's edge, at home with each another's company, and in silence. Someone once told me, "It is in the still, quiet silence that we find God, or we allow ourselves to be found by him." I know the truth of that statement from my time at camp.

Iney's mother, affectionately known as "Granny G," the "G" standing for Gilstrap, her married name, lived the last years of her life at camp in a house made just for her, called "Red Bird Haven." She was known for the gentleness of her spirit, the sharpness of her wit, and her uncanny ability to call birds to her yard, and to even have them land on her shoulder. I recall that her style of clothing gave away her time of birth. She dressed in calico prints and shirtwaist smocks, and she always wore an apron. Her silvery hair was pulled tightly into a bun neatly atop her head. The skin on her hands and face was weathered, marked with tan-colored age spots, and wrinkled from time and all the distances she must have crossed. On warm summer evenings, a dozen or so campers gathered at her feet as she sat in her front yard, enticing red birds near. We waited, awestruck, for a bird to fly in, take its perch, and snap a nibble of cracked corn from her open palm before flying off so quickly that its destination was a mystery.

139

Granny told of the time when she was a mere girl and she had to ride the family mule in from the far pasture because a "blue norther" was approaching. As her trek began, the sky grew ominous. She urged the mule on to a gangly gallop. It must have been a far distance, because by the time she reached the house and barn, the mule's muzzle and whiskers were covered with ice.

She also told a story of planting an old enameled door-knob in a chicken's nest as a decoy. Some old chicken snake would squirm his way into the nest, eat the "egg," and be un-able to slink sway. "Chop him up, wash off that knob as good as new, and use it again," she explained, giggling. Little did we know, as we sat on the carpet grass she had planted dur-ing her ninety-second summer, that we were in the presence of real history. Granny G had lived to cross the prairie in a Conestoga wagon during her girlhood, to the time of the men landing on the moon. She marveled at that fact whenever she saw a full moon, pointing out to us "young-uns," "Who knows what tomorrow will bring."

She was seldom ill in her life, a fact attributed to her hav-ing a "wet nurse" as an infant. Her own mother died shortly after her birth, and she was "raised on that nurse and milk in a whiskey bottle with a turkey quill as a nipple," she said proudly. She created poultices that could "draw a ten penny nail through a two by four," and she read the signs of oncom-ing storms and seasons like a diviner.

She was something of an oddity at camp, an old woman. In an environment filled with youngsters, adolescents, and young adults, her wisdom, wit, and sharp sense of personal determination were in great demand. She was not well edu-cated, she had not traveled coast to coast or abroad, she was never considered a socialite or philanthropist of great renown, yet she had accomplished more in her ninety-six years than most of us ever would in seventy. She birthed eight children right there in her own home, and buried one in infancy. She hoed fields, planted crops, sent her children to bed each night well fed, well scrubbed, and well versed in the message of the "Good Book," and she never complained about anything in her life. She died as she lived: heroically, though largely unknown. She was a woman of true pioneering spirit, with uncommon courage and feistiness. She loved her sons and daughters and at one time fought for the survival of her marriage. She was one of a kind that is, unfortunately, a lost breed. We were lucky to have known such a woman.

If you came upon Granny G unawares, she would sometimes be humming "Amazing Grace" or reciting "How Great Thou Art" to herself. She loved yard work and she used her own push-style lawnmower until the day she accidentally chopped off the end of her big toe. "Oh, well," she said stoically, "I had an ingrown toenail anyways."

Recently I read in Neale Donald Walsch's *Conversations With God: An Uncommon Dialogue, Book 2* something that touched my memory of so many of those heroic people I knew at camp.

When asked, "How do we go about changing the world?" God replies:

Be a light unto the world, and hurt it not. Seek to build, not to destroy.

Bring my people home.

How?

By your shining example. Seek only Godliness. Speak only in truthfulness. Act only in love.

Live the Law of Love now and forevermore. Give everything, require nothing.

Avoid the mundane.

Do not accept the unacceptable.

Teach all who seek to learn of Me.

Make every moment of your life an outpouring of love.

Use every moment to think the highest thought, say the highest word, do the highest deed. In this, glorify your Holy Self, and thus, too, glorify Me.

Bring peace to the earth by bringing peace to all those whose lives touch you.

Be peace.

Feel and express in every moment your Divine Connection with the All, and with every person, place, and thing.

Embrace every circumstance, own every fault, share every joy, contemplate every mystery, walk in every man's shoes, forgive every offense (including your own), heal every

141

heart, honor every person's truth, adore every person's God, protect every person's rights, preserve every person's interests, provide every person's needs, presume every person's holiness, present every person's greatest gifts, produce every person's blessing, and pronounce every person's future secure in the assured love of God.

Be a living, breathing example of the Highest Truth that resides within you.

Speak humbly of yourself, lest someone mistake your highest Truth for a boast.

Speak softly, lest someone think you are merely calling for attention.

Speak gently, that all might know of Love.

Speak openly, lest anyone think you have something to hide.

Speak candidly, so you cannot be mistaken.

Speak often, so that your word may truly go forth.

Speak respectfully, that no one be dishonored.

Speak lovingly, that every syllable may heal.

Speak of Me with every utterance.

Make your life a gift. Remember always, you are the gift!

Be a gift to everyone who enters your life, and to everyone whose life you enter. Be careful not to enter another's life if you cannot be a gift.

(You can always be a gift, because you always are the gift—yet sometimes you don't let yourself know that.)

When someone enters your life unexpectedly, look for the gift that person has come to receive from you . . . .

I tell you this: every person who has ever come to you has come to receive a gift from you. In so doing, he gives a gift to you—the gift of your experiencing and fulfilling Who You Are.

When you see this simple truth, when you understand it, you see the greatest truth of all:

I have sent you nothing but angels. (pp. 175–77)

CHAPTER 13

Philippians 1:3-7; 4:4-9

I thank my God upon every remembrance of you,
Always in every prayer of mine for you all
making request for joy,
For your fellowship in the gospel from the first day until now;
Being confident of this very thing, that he which hath begun a good
work in you will perform it until the day of Jesus Christ:
Even as it is meet for me to think this of you all, because
I have you in my heart; inasmuch as both in my bonds,
and in the defence and confirmation of the gospel, ye all
are partakers of my grace.

Rejoice in the lord always: and again I say, Rejoice.
Let your moderation be known unto all men.
The Lord is at hand.
Be careful for nothing; but in every thing by prayer and supplication
with thanksgiving let your requests be made known unto God.
And the peace of God, which passeth all understanding, shall keep
your hearts and minds through Christ Jesus.
Finally, brethren, whatsoever things are true, whatsoever things are
honest, whatsoever things are just, whatsoever things are pure,
whatsoever things are lovely, whatsoever things are of good report; if
there be any virtue, and if there
be any praise, think on these things.

Recently a friend of mine attended a spiritual retreat at a nearby Benedictine monastery. As time for lunch approached, all gathered around the table, began serving themselves, and started eating. One of the nuns must have noticed the perplexed expression on my friend's face and she asked, "Do you think it is strange that we did not offer grace before the meal?" My friend shrugged, nodded in agreement, and replied, "Well, yes, as a matter of fact." The nuns smiled, and finally one of them explained, "You see we look at everything we do as prayer. Our work, our sleeping, our eating, our sharing together. All of life is a prayer."

It would be truly wonderful if we could all experience every moment of our lives as a sacrament or as a prayer. Each day could be an offering to the God who was gracious enough to grant us the opportunity to see such beauty, witness every act of kindness, and heal all human wounds. Alas, we are human and prone to forgetfulness, self-indulgence, insensitivity, and ego fulfillment. We grab the moments we can. We photograph them and store them away in an album or record them in our journals, and take them out once in a blue moon.

There are times, though, that we are invited to live sacramentally, times that stay forever etched in our memories, lingering there, waiting to be called upon for insight, instruction, or just because we need to relive certain moments now and again. The birth of a child . . . the time of our awakening into adolescence or adulthood . . . graduation . . . marriage . . . these are events that are so powerful in our consciousness that we can experience them again in that unusual state referred to as *déjà vu*. This goes beyond mere memory; it is a sense that *I am there*. In déjà vu, sounds, smells, visions take on the reality of when they were first experienced.

Many may have this experience beyond certain events of their lives; they can recall entire portions of their lives. This is most true in the realm of childhood. When we think of our childhoods, a flood of memories is released, and they come as individual pieces that are part of a whole that may be representative of many years. As I recall my camping years, I see the faces of countless girls whose names I can no longer identify. At once I can become lost in the smell of the river at morning, the smell of new-mowed grass, and especially the odd mixture of smells that seemed to be localized at a spot where Edmund's Creek flowed past the stables and on toward

144

the Flats where it connected with Cypress Creek. At dusk, the summer air had a particular scent that, when combined with the smell of horses, green grass, and the fading heat of the day, made one feel absolutely wistful.

The sounds of those days from time to time fashion round in my head, stirring reverie; the wind strutting across the open water, the call of the night birds, the whirring fans, the strong, steady breathing of dozens of girls inside their cabins. These things have stayed with me. These things have consoled me over the years.

I have not prayed a prayer of thanksgiving each day since camp, but if I had I would have prayed for each and every person, every act, every sunrise and sunset, and every gift that was bestowed on me and others who were blessed by sharing that time in our innocent years. Those days in our childhoods were spent as they were meant to be: long days of daydreaming; sharing dreams and fears in utter sincerity; time to grow physically, mentally, and spiritually; opportunities to watch tadpoles transform themselves, stones try to turn into jelly, and dragonflies stretch their gossamer wings above velvet waters that reflected the very face of God.

Today I am older, but not necessarily wiser. I am, perhaps, more careful, reticent, suspicious, and wary. I have learned the lessons of growing up through some pain of rejection, adjustment, failure, and misplaced dreams. I have not always remembered the lessons I learned long ago on the banks of the Guadalupe River under the care and attention of those who were as needy and as unfamiliar with the world at large as I was. But these things call me. They call me back to a time when I first began to see, and they signal to me that it is time to revisit those long-ago messages, rethink their themes, and put into practice the meaning of their values. *Be ye kind to one another . . . Seek and ye shall find, Knock and it shall be opened unto you . . . We are molded by those that have loved us . . .* and many, many, more.

Can you remember the days of your childhood? Can you recall a time of innocence, a time before you yet understood that some people lie, hurt, or steal? Can you remember a time when you knew God, not because those older had described

145

him to you, or told you stories about him and his mighty works, but remembered him because you had, at one time, known him? Can you wrestle up a memory of when all things were new, and everything was done for the first time? Can you, once again, taste Jell-O for the first time, see your first snowflakes, smell your first puppy, or name your first imaginary friend? We all have these memories stored and locked away someplace in the vast filing cabinets in our minds; the problem is that sometimes it is very difficult, or even unpleasant, to call up those primitive recollections. They may be associated with dark and scary times; times when the Boogey Man lived under the bed or in the closet, times when the dark was a place were you didn't want to see, times when you felt very alone or rejected, or out of place.

Jesus invites us back to that place of childhood where we are loved, and where we are wanted, and where we are safe:

> And they brought young children to him, that he should touch them: and his disciples rebuked those that brought them. But when Jesus saw it, he was much displeased, and said unto them, Suffer the little children to come unto me, and forbid them not: for such is the kingdom of God. Verily I say unto you, Whosoever shall not receive the kingdom of God as a little child, he shall not enter therein. And he took them up in his arms, put his hands upon them, and blessed them. (KJV, Mk. 10:13-16)

This passage from Mark reminds us that we must see God through the eyes of a child if we are to enter into his kingdom, but we are not to stay as children. First, we are encouraged to come gently, peacefully, and full of hope as we seek to encounter God. We meet him like a trusted friend who understands us and does not rush our time together. As we come to know the Lord more intimately, we expand the sacred relationship. Only then do we begin to ask tough questions, seek troubling answers, and strengthen our spiritual foundations. At that point, spiritual maturity begins, and we gain a deeper understanding of the sacred presence, and of the holy path designed for each of us.

I recall again the line from 1 Cornithians, chapter 13,

"But when that which is perfect is come, then that which is in part shall be done away... For now we see through a glass, darkly; but then face to face..." (KJV, 1 Cor. 13:10, 12) It takes time to come to an understanding of God and his involvement in our lives. If we begin the spiritual journey seeking a deep theological, intellectual, or cosmological grasp, we may become quickly lost in cynicism, doubt, and confusion. Come to the Lord first with the openness of a little child, full of trust and eagerness to know and to be in the presence of one with whom you can share love.

There were two books that I first received while at camp that have significantly shaped my thoughts on childhood, innocence, friendship, and, in a symbolic manner, my journey toward faith. One story comes from *The Velveteen Rabbit* by Margery Williams.

> "What is REAL?" asked the Rabbit one day, when they were lying side by side... "Does it mean having things that buzz inside you and a stick-out handle?"
> "Real isn't how you are made," said the Skin Horse. "It's a thing that happens to you. When a child loves you for a long, long time, not just to play with, but REALLY loves you, then you become Real."
> "Does it hurt?" asked the Rabbit.
> "Sometimes," said the Skin Horse, for he was always truthful. "When you are Real you don't mind being hurt."
> "Does it happen all at once, like being wound up," he asked, "or bit by bit?"
> "It doesn't happen all at once," said the Skin Horse. 'You become. It takes a long time. That's why it doesn't happen to people who break easily, or have sharp edges, or who have to be carefully kept. Generally, by the time you are Real, most of your hair has been loved off, and your eyes drop out and you get loose in the joints and very shabby. But these things don't matter at all, because once you are real you can't be ugly, except to people who don't understand."
> (pp. 16-17)

When we are truly loved, by God or by another person, we can never be ugly. As God's love pours over us, our joints are loosened, our outward appearance rubs off, and we be-

147

come like little children again. Have you ever watched two children meet for the first time? They greet shyly, and after a few moments perhaps one of them says, "Would you like to play with me?" The other smiles and says, "Yes," and they are off. There is no need to question who you are, or what do your parents do, or what kind of house you live in, or how much money you have in the bank.

Oscar Hammerstein reminds us of that purity of heart in lines from his famous song from the musical *South Pacific:* "You have to be taught to love and to hate. You have to be taught before it's too late. You have to be carefully taught."

The story of the Little Prince who is "tamed" by the fox is another favorite that has powerful meaning in my life. Antoine De Saint-Exupery weaves his mystical message:

> "Good morning," said the fox.
> "Good morning," the little prince responded politely . . .
> "Who are you?" asked the little prince, and added, "You are very pretty to look at."
> "I am a fox," the fox said.
> "Come and play with me," proposed the little prince . . .
> "I cannot play with you," the fox said. "I am not tamed."
> . . . "What does that mean—'tame.'"
> . . . "It means to establish ties" . . . "To me, you are still nothing more than a little boy who is just like a hundred thousand other little boys. And I have no need of you. And you, on your part, have no need of me. To you, I am nothing more than a fox like a hundred thousand other foxes. But if you tame me, then we shall need each other. To me, you will be unique in all the world. To you, I shall be unique in all the world . . ."
> "I am beginning to understand . . .
> [And the fox said] . . . if you tame me, it will be as if the sun came to shine on my life. I shall know the sound of a step that will be different from all the others. Other steps send me hurrying back underneath the ground. Yours will call me like music, out of my burrow. And then look: you see the grain-fields down yonder . . . you have hair that is the color of gold. Think how wonderful that will be when you have tamed me! The grain, which is also golden, will bring

148

me back the thought of you. And I shall love to listen to the wind in the wheat.

... "What must I do, to tame you? Asked the little prince.

"You must be very patient," replied the fox.

And later, as they are departing from one another, the fox says:

"And now here is my secret, a very simple secret: It is only with the heart that one can see rightly; what is essential is invisible to the eye." (pp. 64-67, 70)

The Little Prince's secret is one shared by children, by steadfast friends, and by those who love God. Children accept the mysterious as ordinary, and that is why faith comes easily to them. They have the uncanny ability to see with their hearts, rather than with the oftentimes judgmental eyes of one who needs to make a good impression.

Spiritual writer Macrina Wiederkehr invites us on a sacred journey in *Season of Your Heart: Prayers and Reflections*, reminding us that we must walk with the simplicity and energy of a child.

There is a *child* in us who must stay alive if we are to grow in holiness. It is the same child Jesus placed in our midst when he told us that we could hardly expect to handle heaven unless we become like that child. The tired adult in us often needs to be reminded that we are in charge of that child. You and I have the power to let it live or to bring about its early death. And so, my much-too-adult heart challenges you today: Go set free someone else's child by believing in your own ... (p. 21)

Wiederkehr recalls for all of us that time, that need, that longing:

Once upon a time
when days were still fresh
and new,
ordinary
and uncomplicated,

149

I was a free child
in love with everything...
   a bee buzzing
   the wind in my hair
   a branch to hang from
   bare feet in the grass
   dandelions and fairies
   teddy bears.
I don't remember growing up.
It must have happened while I wasn't looking
but it is obvious from my heart
that it has happened
for I am less simple
more complicated
and more cluttered.
   I would not choose
   to become a child again
   but I am looking to children
   and searching in them
   for a simplicity and ordinariness
   that makes being an adult
   easier to accept
   and miracles easier to see.
Children are not too sophisticated
to wonder
to take off their shoes
to reach out, and up
and all around
for that's where miracles are.
   The child in me longs
   to touch all of the adults I know
   with the magic wand of littleness
   and perform that great miracle
   of enabling them to understand
   that it's not too late
   to live happily ever after.
   The problem is so simple
   they could miss it.
   Their teddy bears

they've thrown too far
and how desperately they need them. (pp. 21-22)

There have been times over the last twenty years when I desperately needed to find that child within me. Times when my adult self had failed me or when other adults had ceased to console me. It was at those times that my memories served me well by returning me to that time and place where all seemed so simple and abundant. Living close to nature has been that place of solace for me also. Living close to the land, gardening, and working with horses and other companion animals has taught me about unconditional love, the necessary exchange between those who depend on one another, and a sense of my place within the world I have made for myself.

I had a dream not long after my last summer at camp. I was walking across a wide, open, lush meadow with friends from camp and family, most notably Iney and Frank, my grandparents, and hundreds of those faces I can still recall from my time at Mystic. We strolled happily through the ankle-deep grass, laughing and talking, but I was somehow always at the front of the crowd, not as though I was leading them, but because it was my journey. Soon we reached a beautiful mountain, a monolith covered in green grass. It loomed high into the clouds with a well-worn path ascending to the top.

At first, many from the crowd followed behind me as I climbed, but at the steps grew steeper, many stopped, waited, and looked upward. I became more and more breathless and exhausted with each step, but Iney and Frank, and my grandparents, and a few dear friends remained close behind. As I looked up I could see the path winding up and around and growing more narrow. Soon it was only wide enough for one person at a time to pass.

Finally the path flattened out slightly, and as I paused to look down, I could see the great expanse of grassland, flowering meadow, and multitudes of people below. I was not afraid, but I knew instinctively that I must continue on the journey alone.

I said to those nearby, "You can't go with me anymore. I must go the rest of the way by myself. I have to do this alone."

They watched without emotion as I turned to go. I walked on toward the summit and into the clouds.

This dream has stayed with me with extraordinary clarity for more than twenty years. It spoke of a time in my life when I was ready, however reluctantly, to go on to another phase, another horizon. I was prepared to leave behind the things of childhood and to go alone toward the future. The crowd in my dream consisted of all those people and all those events that had been instrumental in my formation to that point. As I climbed the mountain alone, I had in my possession the necessary tools for the journey: a sense of joy and wonder, a feeling of self-confidence, friends to rely on, and a background (the lovely meadow) that was filled with beautiful memories.

Noted mythologist and teacher Joseph Campbell states that we must all venture forth on our journey in an effort to know ourselves authentically:

> we have not even to risk the adventure alone, for the heroes of all time have gone before us. The labyrinth is thoroughly known. We have only to follow the thread of the hero path, and where we had thought to find an abomination, we shall find a god. And where we had thought to slay one another, we shall slay ourselves. Where we had thought to travel outward, we will come to the center of our own existence. And where we had thought to be alone, we will be with all the world. (p. 123)

Campbell explains the ancient Arthurian myth of the search for the Holy Grail in *Transformations of Myth Through Time*. Sir Gawain set out upon his quest for the Holy Grail with other Knights of the Round Table. They decided it would be more honorable to go alone, rather than as a group. Each one determined at what point they would enter the forest. They would not begin their journeys together, or at the same place, but they did agree to enter "where it was darkest and there was no path." (p. 211) The knights dared not choose someone else's path for the greatest journey of their lives. Each had to make his own way, even though his chosen path might be full of disasters, calamity, suffering, and even death. During the quest, a few of the knights do retreat from their own way and

152

begin to follow the steps of another knight. Bad mistake! Each time this happens, they go astray and complicate their situation. The message is that each one of us must, eventually, make our own way in this life, else we risk becoming part of what T. S. Eliot called "the vast wasteland." Eliot's wasteland was not a barren desert. No, it was the place of inauthenticity, the place where you lose yourself by becoming what others think you should be, or tell you to be.

Granny G was famous for a saying: "Everybody's got to go over Fool's Hill once in their lives. The trick is to make it over without ruining their lives." We go over Fool's Hill alone. Perhaps we follow someone else over that hill, but usually we wander up to that place where we test ourselves, stretch the limits, make a few mistakes, and, hopefully, learn enough from them that we don't go up that hill again. I've been up Fool's Hill . . . more than once. I have survived because I had something calling me home, assuring me of those things I have always known to be true.

There were others I knew at camp who made their own journeys up Fool's Hill. Most ventured that way more than once. Some almost didn't make it back. A few were lost. Happily, most of us were reminded of something that stopped us in our tracks, showed us the error of our ways, and lovingly led us down the path to self.

Years after their camp days, many women have driven down that familiar path past Senior Hill, across Cypress Creek, and on to the Flats. They have walked alongside the waters of Natural Fountains and found their way to the sacred tribe hills of their youth, in search of answers: "Who am I? What has happened to me, to my marriage, to my children? Why was everything so simple here? Where is God?" They long to hear again familiar songs: "Peace I ask of thee, O river . . . . There was a gal that I once knew, by the name of Slew Foot Sue . . . . White coral bells along a slender stalk . . . . Purple lights, on the canyon, purple lights, I long to see." Maybe there are answers in those voices. Perhaps the familiar landscape will comfort us.

Some have brought boyfriends or fiancés to this place, trying to introduce them to a part of themselves that was forgotten long ago, but not actually lost. Many have been healed simply by sitting on the stone steps of Chapel Hill, looking out across and back into time and themselves.

What is the healing power of memory? Is it that it transports us back into a time and place where we are able to single out significant messages or experiences, and then translate them to our current needs? I do not know for sure. Yet, whenever I return to that landscape, no matter the season, I am reminded of people, voices, moments, and expressions that linger, come alive again, and play out before me like an old movie. I stop for a moment, close my eyes, take in a deep breath, and see from where I have come. Once I read that "I am a part of all I see, and all I have seen is a part of whatever I shall become." Like a patchwork, I am made of differing fabrics cut in varying sizes and shapes. The stitches that bind the pieces that are me have been carefully and gently sewn. I have had good teachers. Whether they knew it or not, they were efficient, dutiful, and wise. I cannot remember the names of some, and others I can recall with such clarity that I can almost touch them. They have taught me faith. They have shown me love. They have held my hand when I was most in need of support, and they have urged me forward when I wanted to stand still.

I hope that I have touched some lives in ways that have been meaningful. I trust that I am a part of someone's memories and that they recall me by name, or by impression, with a smile and with gratitude. We can never truly say good-bye to what is our past. We may try to forget, to press those recollections down under to a place where it is difficult, if not impossible, to unearth them. But that is not always the best way to lock away the past, however painful or troublesome our memories may be.

The time of leaving camp was most difficult, not only for the campers and counselors and staff, but for the parents, too. Those closing days of summer were a time of personal re-adjustment; campers back to house rules and school, counselors back to college and prospects of their future, staff returning to current jobs and families. Only the land remained and rested, now quiet, alone, and still. It settles in for a change of season: the blue-green waters of the river turn blue-black as the winds begin to chill, the tiny green needles of the cypress trees grow brittle and tawny, the leaves of Spanish oak wear gold, russet, and ginger, and it isn't long before the lonely wind howls around empty cabins and naked trees. All that remains breathes a sigh of contentment. Rest . . . Renew . . . Refresh . . . until in the early spring, from deep within the earth, something signals that it is time for beginning again. The ritual dance of preparation is inaugurated. Nature is fast at work, changing bare limbs to boughs full of color and lace; dry brown straw is replaced with soft green loam. Baby cottontails nest near the home plate on the unmowed softball field. Tiny armadillos are already learning their rooting techniques and terrorizing those who care for the immaculate golf greens. Fawns stand on spindly legs but soon learn to leap and jump, defying gravity and definitions of beauty in nature.

And far away in the corner of some room is a little girl packing her trunk with T-shirts, red shorts, flashlight, stuffed animal, and stationary for chicken letters to home. She is impatient with the season, anxious for summer. She can already hear the camp songs; she hums them to herself. She dreams of riding horses up Bald Mountain, and eating s'mores by a blazing campfire. What will she learn this summer? What lifelong friends will she find? How will God, and a love of nature, and a respect for others find their way deeper into her heart?

She has an open heart, not yet cluttered with false trinkets from the world. She greets the day and all that unfolds within it with arms outstretched. She is going to camp. She is communing with the season, summer. I remember when she was me. Do you remember when she was you?

Finally, brethren, farewell. Be perfect, be of good comfort,
be of one mind, live in peace;
and the God of love and peace shall be with you.
Greet one another with an holy kiss.
All the saints salute you.
The grace of the Lord Jesus Christ, and the love of God,
and the communion of the Holy Ghost, be with you all. Amen.
(KJV, 2 Cor. 13:11–14)

Bibliography

Breathnach, Sarah Ban, *Simple Abundance: A Daybook of Comfort and Joy* (New York: Time Warner Books, 1995).

Campbell, Joseph, *The Power of Myth* (New York: Doubleday, 1988).

———, *Transformations of Myth Through Time* (New York: Harper and Row, 1990).

D'Arcy, Paula, *The Gift of the Red Bird: A Spiritual Encounter* (New York: Crossroads Publishing, 1998).

Friedman, Maurice, *To Deny Our Nothingness* (Chicago, Ill.: University of Chicago Press, 1978).

Kushner, Harold S., *When Bad Things Happen To Good People* (New York: Schocken Books, 1981).

L'Engle, Madeleine, *Walking On Water: Reflections on Faith and Art* (Wheaton, Ill.: Harold Shaw Publishers, 1980).

Moore, Thomas, *The Re-Enchantment of Everyday Life* (New York: HarperCollins, 1996).

The NIV/KJV Parallel Bible (Grand Rapids, Michigan: Zondervan Bible Publishers, 1983).

Norris, Kathleen, *Amazing Grace: A Vocabulary of Faith* (New York: Riverhead Books, 1998).

O'Donohue, John, *Eternal Echoes: Exploring our Yearning to Belong* (New York: Cliff Street Books, 1999).

Pintauro, Joseph, and Sister Corita Kent, *To Believe in God* (New York: Harper and Row, 1968).

Saint-Exupery, Antoine De, *The Little Prince* (New York: Harcourt, Brace and World, 1943).

Sullivan, Claudia, *Summer Come, Summer Go: A Collection of Memories* (Austin, Texas: Nortex Press, 1991).

Toor, Djohariah, *The Road By the River* (New York: St. Martin's Press, 1987).

Walsch, Neale Donald, *Conversations with God: An Uncommon Dialogue, Book 2* (Charlottesville, Virginia: Hampton Road Publishing Company, 1997).

Wiederkehr, Macrina, O.S.B., *Seasons of Your Heart* (San Francisco, Calif.: Harper, 1985).

Wilder, Thornton, *Our Town* (New York: Coward-McCann, 1938).

Williams, Margery, *The Velveteen Rabbit: Or How Toys Become Real* (Garden City, New York: Doubleday and Company, 1971).

www.ingramcontent.com/pod-product-compliance
Lightning Source LLC
Chambersburg PA
CBHW060051100426
42742CB00014B/2785